In the Blue Pharmacy

Also by Marianne Boruch

—Poetry—

Poems New and Selected

A Stick that Breaks and Breaks

Moss Burning

Descendant

View from the Gazebo

—Prose—

Poetry's Old Air

Marianne Boruch

In the
Blue Pharmacy

*Essays on Poetry and
Other Transformations*

Trinity University Press
San Antonio

Published by Trinity University Press
San Antonio, Texas 78212

Cover design by BookMatters, Berkeley
Book design by Jennifer Kelly-DeWitt, BookMatters

⊗ The paper used in this publication meets the minimum requirements of the
American National Standard for Information Sciences—Permanence of Paper for
Printed Library Materials, ANSI Z39.48-1992.

Library of Congress Cataloging-in-Publication Data

Boruch, Marianne, 1950–
In the blue pharmacy : essays on poetry and other transformations /
Marianne Boruch.
p. cm.
"Sixteen essays on poets and poetry, the writing life, and how the
imagination works with mystery and surprise in a variety of poets from
Elizabeth Bishop to Theodore Roethke"—Provided by publisher.
Includes bibliographical references and index.
ISBN 1-59534-010-6 (hardcover : alk. paper)—ISBN 1-59534-011-4 (pbk. : alk. paper)
1. Poetry. 2. PoetryAuthorship. 3. American poetry—History and criticism.
I. Title.
PS3552.07564515 2005
808.1—dc22   2004029740
09   08   07   06   05   5   4   3   2   1

In memory of Elinor Brogden,
beloved cousin

Contents

Acknowledgments   *ix*

Line and Room   1
Decoys   19
Williams and the Bomb   37
Poets in Cars   53

Edson's Head   75
The Shape of His Melancholy   81
Three Spirits   87
Becoming "Epithalamion"   93
Rhetoric and Mystery   101
Two Veils   107
Original Shell   115
The End of a Century   123

Worlds Old and New   131
Bishop's Blue Pharmacy   151
Poetry's Over and Over   164
The Rage to Reorder   183

Works Consulted   207
Index   215

Acknowledgments

I'm grateful to the editors of the following journals for first publishing these pieces, all in a slightly earlier form: the *Iowa Review* ("Decoys" and "Worlds Old and New"); *American Poetry Review* ("Williams and the Bomb" and "Poetry's Over and Over"); *Michigan Quarterly Review* ("Line and Room"); *New England Review/ Breadloaf Quarterly* ("Bishop's Blue Pharmacy"); *Massachusetts Review* ("Poets in Cars"), *Indiana Review* ("Edson's Head"); and *Field* ("The Shape of His Melancholy," "Three Spirits," "Original Shell," "Rhetoric and Mystery," "Becoming 'Epithalamion,'" and "Two Veils"). These last six pieces were written by invitation, and my thanks go especially to editors David Young, Stuart Friebert, and David Walker for thinking of me for their symposia, the first five of these essays appearing also in *Poets Reading: The FIELD Symposia* (Oberlin College Press, 1999). "The End of the Century" was written for the tribute to Tom Andrews chaired by David Young at the 2004 Associated Writing Programs annual meeting. It also appeared on the Oberlin College Press Web site. The essay "Worlds Old and New" was first published, in a briefer incarnation, in *Falling Toward Grace: Images of Religion and Culture in One American City* (Indiana University Press, 1998), and "Poets in Cars" was reprinted on the Web site *Poetry Daily* in 2004. I'm grateful as well to the presses that first published the eight poems I've written closely about here.

Many thanks to those who aided in my learning about areas these essays touch, especially when I drifted beyond the subject of poetry. The list is long and includes David Lewis, Archival Librarian at the Indiana State Library in Indianapolis; Lois Himelick at the Indianapolis Symphony Orchestra Library; Mabel Webb at the Athenaeum, also in that city. Closer to home, there's Pat DeFlaun, Randy Woodson, Wendy Flory, Mary Nieopukj, Barbara Bean, Dorothy Deering, Helen Brown, Lesha Hurliman, Martin Curd, Regan Eckstein, and Margo Marlatt. I'm also grateful to David Hamilton for his comments, and to Herbert Leibowitz for his, especially reminding me of Williams's poem "The Sparrow" as I worked on "The Rage to Reorder." In the last months, as I put this collection together, I was generously aided by Susan Neville, Brigit Kelly, Ellen Voigt, and especially Joy Manesiotis. Continuing thanks, of course, to my patient editor, poet Barbara Ras.

I owe a huge debt to the MFA Program at Warren Wilson College, the very supportive students and faculty there who provided the occasion for all but two of the longer essays here, which were first written as lectures. I want to acknowledge the National Endowment for the Arts, and Purdue's Center for Artistic Endeavors for the fellowships and the Department of English at Purdue for the sabbatical, all of which allowed me time to work on these essays as well as on poems. The English department? Of course I need to mention with warm gratitude my students and colleagues there for their good company and insight in our ongoing discussions of poetry.

Finally, how to thank these two enough? My husband and son, David and Will Dunlap, who shared their irreverent wisdom in all things regarding this book, and beyond. What luck I've had to know their steady, good-hearted encouragement, day after day after day.

LINE AND ROOM

The first act of movement (line)
takes us far beyond the dead point.
—*Paul Klee*

A   group
of   students
passed   the
House —
one   of them
said   Oh
no   like you
the   same
vagabond
sweetness
I   followed the
      voice
—*Emily Dickinson*

To line bees: To track wild bees
to their nest by following their
line of flight.

Among the astonishing things Thomas Edison helped manage in his
lifetime—incandescent light, the phonograph, the electric chair—
was a curious book, compiled by others and published in 1940, sev-
enteen years after his death. A small part is his diary—entries from ten

largely eventless July days in 1885—and the rest, written after retirement, falls in place as "Sundry Observations" on everything: his life, the world's war and peace, the "realms beyond." I've never been to a Chautauqua camp meeting, but it's possible his remarks fit its heyday mold—rambling, quirky, mildly inflammatory, moralistic, and often surprisingly boring because there is no self-doubt in the rendering. Yet fascinating, too, because of that, particularly when he takes on the larger world. The inventor at such moments invents that world; he imagines he *speaks out.*

But there are quieter times when Edison seems to be talking to himself. His deafness, gradually increasing throughout his life, may be the central fact about him. He begins his observations recounting the fabled boyhood incident, being lifted by the ears into a moving train by a well-meaning conductor. Elsewhere he dramatizes this moment—"I felt something snap inside my head"—though not here. Because here the issue isn't complaint or self-pity but the realization of a gift, a gift that would save him from a lifetime of stifling small talk, not to mention business-lunch oratory, though there were even happier consequences. He would lean closer, earlier than propriety might dictate, to the woman he would marry; he would come to love New York, to him "a rather quiet place," Broadway "a peaceful thoroughfare." Years of the gift would calm his nerves. "I am able to write without tremor," he claimed. "Few men my age can do that."

His changes went further, moving him inward. Thanks to his deafness, he actually thought differently, he said, solitude always available to him, a state he preferred anyway. When he did manage to hear, he would hear exactly in reverse, where others could not, catching ordinary talk in boiler rooms without trouble because the general brain-numbing racket was, literally, nothing to him; or eavesdropping on women across the aisle in roaring trains "telling secrets to one another, taking advantage of the noise" which, unknown to them, only Edison could screen out. As for his early fascination with the telegraph: "Deafness was an advantage. While I could hear unerringly the loud ticking of the instrument, I would not hear other sounds. I could not even hear the instrument of the man next to me in the big office." In that room, an island of quiet then; one imagines the beat from the incoming wire, two beats, three and four. Pauses held and let go, a meaningful rhythm. Bad news or good news, grief or love or both. So much like the making of a poem suddenly, the poet alert, waiting to translate something from somewhere, the whole private business. Edison bent over it. Edison writing the words as they come great distances across the river or across the world. From some far-away room there, probably equal in size, with a window or two, though its quiet can't be equal.

As if anything is equal. Not Edison, really, not like a poet at all I suppose, though his solitude might serve and shine here, or the way, in writing poems, lines often come unbidden. Voices up from where though? What ancient room in us, and why the line and not the sentence? And what of lines end-stopped as opposed to enjambed? Is it the difference, as Edison might understand it, between electricity's habits? Direct current—its DC—like so many an end-stopped line, runs its brief charge straight, no tricks, to begin and end sensibly enough, while AC—alternating current—seems to enjamb itself, circling then hitting resistance to reverse its charge, endlessly restless, going whatever distance to light a room or a *stanza*, the Italian word for room.

Or is the poetic line mere artifice, ornament, an aid to memory, end-rhymed so often in the past for that? And why do lines obsess those who write them, Tennyson, say—as my colleague Dorothy Deering tells me—using "The phantom circle of a moaning sea" repeatedly in drafts of different poems, always crossing it out until finally one year, in "The Passing of Arthur," it fit? Or is this fracturing just rote and we long ago lost its reason because poetry is written like that, thank you, and prose is not, and we learn this fact early the way a child learns the order of a day, sleep at either end, or gardeners learn to plant in rows because to weed, one has to stand or kneel somewhere. Whatever the cause, sentences get broken into lines; we thread them down—of course, from the Latin *linea*, meaning "linen"—this way, that way, as the word *verse* whose root *vertere*, "to turn," reminds us, the way a kid's marble run might work, the structure itself urging each burst, or because we're drawn to the senseless on/off rush of it though probably nothing is entirely random. "The things I needed to hear," Edison, who could barely make out anything, assures us, "I have heard."

One needs to hear in the line, what exactly? As opposed to gregarious prose whose public purpose assumes audience—to tell a story, to give direction, to admit to murder—poems don't *do* things. They're solitary, the young telegraph man praising his deafness because it cut him off from the silly supper gossip at the boarding house so he could think—or dream, years later, he *was* thinking. It's just that the speakers of poems so often talk to themselves or to some other so close it might as well be the self. Intimate guardians of those crucial human nothings: to resist or brood or lament, to declare love or take it back. Not that these genre differences are new. There's always Yeats's idea of poetry as one's argument with oneself while rhetoric, if not all prose, is busy elsewhere, taking on the world. Under such distinctions, even the sonnet has been elevated in this age that scorns it, redefined recently by Paul Oppenheimer, who makes it evidence, as his book's title suggests, of "the birth of the modern mind," finding through that first sonnet somewhere in the twelfth century the actual moment humankind looked inward to record the famous argument with the self, to hell with the world—or at least to hell with the lute and the idea of performing a poem in front of all those people at the court.

If poetry is our literary form of solitude, our way back to that most private of rooms, then its deepest architecture—its controlling tension—depends on line. Perhaps this drama between poetry and

prose enacts itself within every poem, particularly if the line's enjambed. Enter Edison once more, bent close to his telegraph, screen-
ing out the world's cacophony to focus, line by line. Which is to say,
it's the public, talkative sentence out there or its near-brother, the
lucid fragment, each with syntax's reasonable complexity and both
to be refigured brutally, if elegantly, by the line as it breaks to another
line. Brooks and Warren said it memorably: the sentence is a unit of
sense but the line is a unit of attention. A way of foregrounding what
really matters, I'd guess, a way of steadying things. And what of the
world beyond, larger than the sentence and its logic, the daily confusion out of which all art comes? Two philosophers—Deleuze and
Guattari—define chaos not so much as disorder but as "the infinite
speed with which every form taking shape in it vanishes." Line as a
still, then, against life's dizzying momentum which, at heart, is the
lyric impulse anyway, to stop time, to feel the eternal weight of what
is ordinary, or maybe just to breathe slower. Sometimes even what is
flippant turns grave by such choreography. "What a thrill——" Plath
writes in these first few lines from her poem "Cut,"

> My thumb instead of an onion.
> The top quite gone
> Except for a sort of a hinge
>
> Of skin,
> A flap like a hat,
> Dead white.
> Then that red plush.

Plath, of course, had greater monsters before her. Another poem,
"Elm," written in the same year as "Cut," just months before her
death, eerily places long, languid lines against briefer ones as in these
opening stanzas.

I know the bottom, she says. I know it with my great tap root:
It is what you fear.
I do not fear it: I have been there.

Is it the sea you hear in me,
Its dissatisfactions?
Or the voice of nothing, that was your madness?

Love is a shadow.
How you lie and cry after it
Listen: these are its hooves: it has gone off, like a horse.

All night I shall gallop thus, impetuously,
Till your head is a stone, your pillow a little turf,
Echoing, echoing.

Or shall I bring you the sound of poisons?
This is rain now, this big hush.
And this is the fruit of it: tin-white, like arsenic.

"Elm" carries Plath's purest form of nightmare, not distanced by irony for once though deflected by a mask of sorts, half extended metaphor, half fable. The tree seems, at times, to speak its own horrors, the poet somewhere behind, speaking hers. But poetic shape here, lines that lock and unlock, suggests a rich strain in countless ways throughout the piece. Her lines, when end-stopped by period, comma, or question mark, shore up energy then release it, a dirgelike cadence that adds dignity, a way to control a situation largely out of control. As the vision gradually darkens, enjambment increases, that earlier *wrought* quality of the end-stops slipping now, one line then another overflowing into the next.

I keep going back to the opening line, two sentences with every calm in the world about them. Plath gives it to us straight. "I know the bottom, she says. I know it with my great tap root." But its power depends on the next step, as suddenly a second line is formed, under-scoring what can only be called forbidden knowledge. "It is what you fear," she tells us flatly, unblinkingly. Such words say what they say in full light; their "sentence sound," that ordinary, ongoing cadence that Frost named and loved in poems, seems reasonable enough. But the physical pull downward, enacted by the end line pause, is what takes us without warning into the nether world. It is *line* in the poem that amplifies threat to make this more chilling. Donald Hall was right to praise the line for its instant connection to our "psychic interior," access one feels through the body, through "mouth and muscle." "I am terrified by this dark thing / That sleeps in me," Plath writes else-where in the piece, "All day I feel its soft, feathery turnings, its malig-nity." Lines in fact break far more than sentences. Here, they break down the weight of her fevered realizations so it becomes possible—or bearable—to take them in. Even so, it's all rush and dread as line gives way to each line below, until the fiercest solitude fills up the room. Until there is no room.

Start again, then, and say the obvious, that once we've passed into such interiors it seems impossible to speak with precision. In describ-ing line, after all, one describes what Charles Simic calls "the most intuitive part of the writing process." What's *heard* is only part of the mystery. Their presence is visual too, how lines live in space to idle there and pull back, far from margins. Line comes this way from Euclid, to him from Plato who described it as "a breathless length," or so I read recently in Euclid's *Elements*—misread, really—thrilled, everything else in my head happily abandoned for a second. Not breathing, I thought: *a breathless length*. In fact, it was *breadthless* I read, this slip without weight, length without volume, line pure enough for every shape in the world. But one can misread and find truth, at least a memory of truth, thirty years back for me, to Euclid's book in a classroom, the oldest nun in the world at the board, gumming her words, then staring out past trees, forgetting us. And what relief to hover there at our desks in the quiet above his proofs, the lines of argument following, making sense, how each froze that order too, one line set then released by the next, down the page until the last second's *therefore* came right out of dream—a door flung open where you never thought there'd be a room, secret under the house where you never thought anything secret.

How sight and sound actually connect—poetry as *figure*, moving because the eye moves: this has been the bothersome issue since print or, before that, since we started to write things down, line always the place where spatial and auditory elements cross. That is, where space and time cross. One sees it and one hears it. Perhaps more eerily, one *sees it coming* and *sees where it's been* even in the most cursory glance at the page, lines—the overall shape they make—the first thing we probably notice about poems. There are more ancient beginnings to this. Those who study maps back to prehistory tell us that the grassland habits of homo sapiens, so different from the forest primates, forced a first, crucial aspect of human consciousness—to see spatially, to know distance as it links to heartstop matters of safety and fear. And wonder too, I imagine, the world in a blink opened like that, an *expanse*, as if we've never lived on the earth at all but float above it always with a godlike, generalizing eye. As for those ancestral grasslands that spawned such a view—survival, as the historian G. Malcolm Lewis put it, depended on our developing at the same time both prospect and refuge, that is, vision and self-concealment. In short, to look without being seen. To open and to close at once.

In truth, I love these two unlikely worlds together. They seem perfect sisters, birder that I am, sitting these summer mornings an hour or two in open places because I prize my prospect of the woods' edge from there. My concealment is stillness, waiting and looking without gesture until even the shrewdest tanager thinks I'm some weird badly pruned holly bush or some harmless debris left by a fugitive midnight truck. A line, said Paul Klee in his days teaching at the German Bauhaus, is a topographical measurement of the journey we take. But how to measure my stillness against what I hear, the ecstatic thrush, hidden, thrilling in the ragged low branches. How even to try.

Fact: when poets exchange old concealments for new concealments, their lines change. Much of early Roethke, for instance, resembles later Roethke, well, not at all, except perhaps in subject matter, as praise of the natural world's hard disorder and our place in it. The best thing about "Long Live the Weeds" from his first book, *Open House*, is probably its title, a direct—if admitted—steal from Hopkins. Its shape, though, has almost nothing in common with the Jesuit's fresh, edgy rhythms or even Roethke's later sound. "Long live the weeds that overwhelm / my narrow vegetable realm!" he begins in a deliberate burst.

> The bitter rock, the barren soil
> That force the son of man to toil;
> All things unholy, marred by curse,
> The ugly of the universe.
> The rough, the wicked, and the wild
> That keep the spirit undefiled.

And so on, in the shadow of Pope or Milton of a tidier age. But the even stress here—mainly four beats against an occasional three—invites to the poem little of the wildness spoken of, the end rhymes too expected, and—do I say it?—almost smug. When all's too safe, it's danger we look for, charged by whatever long buried gene from our years as primates just out of the forest and onto the grasslands, scanning the terrain; it's probably habit by now, our alertness to uncertainty, to things different. But Roethke's lines gather like good soldiers, moving their pronouncements down trench to trench, sure of themselves in the old end-stopped way with little relief from the burgherdom they serve except perhaps in the monkey-wrench penultimate line, unstable because it's five stresses now, the poet hoping that his sympathy for things uneven earns him more daring moments to "hope, love, create, or drink and die."

Such moments come closer with his second collection, *The Lost Son*, poems less *comment upon* and more about experience, open season now on real memories of a Michigan childhood caught between his father's orderly greenhouses and stranger places. In fact, foreshadowing the growth in longer later poems, Roethke's sense of poetic shape changes with that book. The old concealment of an elegant, generalizing distance is going and with it the *step to* sound of things cut and stressed so evenly. We're out of a box and into a larger, less organized room. Here is the title poem's much looser start.

> At Woodlawn I heard the dead cry:
> I was lulled by the slamming of iron,
> A slow drip over stones,
> Toads brooding wells.
> All the leaves stuck out their tongues;
> I shook the softening chalk of my bones,
> Saying,
> Snail, snail, glister me forward,
> Bird, soft-sigh me home,
> Worm, be with me.

Roethke's end-stop habit continues here, not to mention his respect for the sentence and, in turn, the line as syntactic unit. These things add to the classic integrity of his work in part because, as Frost liked to quote Yvor Winters, "behind all good free verse there's a shadow of formal verse," in which, certainly, Roethke was expert.

All that isn't said here is heard—and seen—as well. It's Roethke mapping more intimate ground in highly visual ways, both prospect and refuge coming because he's mapped silence and hesitation right into the line. "I shook the softening chalk of my bones / saying"—but the line goes dead and we wait too, idling until the whisper is dropped to the next line. "Snail, snail, glisten me forward, / Bird, soft-sigh me home." So Roethke fills and staggers and questions and comes up quick, the full piece an assemblage of voices and styles. To vary things, especially line length, shows how the mind actually moves, he wrote later. More than that, in this first passage, his short lines against more willowy ones, his repeated direct address to soothe and quiet things, make a different kind of concealment, a stepping back even as the tone of the piece grows bolder, more personal. One *sees* it taking place; line is physical gesture too.

I hesitate to call this *method*. Nevertheless, an analogy: each fall, I bicycle past the surveying class at Purdue, kids with their scopes and twine, year after year measuring the same acre of open space, setting down stakes, drawing the cord taut between them. But beyond this over-calculated corner, there are jagged edges in the world, squiggles on a map where ponds begin, river and creek banks, messy coastlines of rock and sand. For this, surveyors have invented the so-called "meander line," measured at the mean high-water mark and drawn more to approximate than to be accurate, to generalize the measure-less dips and turns that a boundary of rock and mud and water makes. Such ecstasies aside, I'm thinking more often about the free-verse line in this way, especially the enjambed line that moves in two directions, restlessly *across* then cutting *down* to surprise or deflect or underscore. A romantic invention, enjambment, impressing the Elizabethans, then scorned in the eighteenth century, as Roger Mitchell has pointed out, but picked up again with wild love by the real romantics of the next century, throughout history a creature of messier, more uncertain—more *meandering*—times.

More recently these *meander lines*, which slow or stop suddenly to reflect the near viscous depth of things, have gotten stranger, certainly more visual. I'd include Jorie Graham in this, thinking of an older collection, *The End of Beauty*, her third, because like Roethke's second book, it mapped a dramatic shift in direction, altering established points of refuge and prospect. Here, in a passage from her poem "The Lovers," a fitful interior movement is mimed by a new set of structural eccentricities. "Either they are or they're not, she thinks, hold still," Graham writes.

> Something fiery all around—let it
>   decide.
> It will need us to shape it (won't it?)   hold still.
> And the cries increasingly   hold still.
> Like a _____ this look between us   hold still.
> If, inside, a small terrified happiness begins
> like an idea of color
> like an idea of color sinking to stain an instance, a *thing*,
> like an arm holding a lit candle in a door that is parting,
> if, oh if—banish it.
> Listen, this is the thing that can trap it now—the glance—

More than Roethke, Graham forces her line to follow an inside fury, pent up and thus increased through her curious breaks and midline blanks. Their looming up so clearly on the page suggests process, not the truth but a groping for it though mainly, like Roethke, she holds to the well-mannered sentence as the basic understructure. Perhaps line has become more subtle a tracking device this way, words unfolding haltingly, their placement on the page equally telling.

A sea change like Graham's, like Roethke's, from a more conventional line to this looser translation, is almost itself a convention in our time. Adrienne Rich comes to mind, or James Wright. A well-known story is Lowell's, which amounted to a conversion of sorts, from his dense, highly metrical and rhetorical line in earlier books to *Life Studies*, which broke nearly everything open. To Lowell, the change seemed enormous, altering even his take on poems he once learned and loved. "Now that I've joined you in unscanned verse," wrote William Carlos Williams just before *Life Studies* came out, "I am struck by how often the old classics get boxed up in their machinery, the sonority of the iambic pentameter line."

Lowell's old machinery sounds like this, from his first book, a middle passage from "The Quaker Graveyard in Nantucket":

Whenever winds are moving and their breath
Heaves at the roped-in bulwarks of this pier,
The terns and sea-gulls tremble at your death
In these home waters. Sailor, can you hear
The Pequod's sea wings, beating landward, fall
Headlong and break on our Atlantic wall. . . .

And later machinery? His work in *Life Studies* shows reach as well as limits. His devotion to rhyme, to things predictable and in pattern, continues in a poem like "Skunk Hour," but second thoughts and hesitations are recorded as well, line breaks governed without punctuation and often with ellipses, things one needs to see to understand. The stops and starts that express vulnerability so poignantly help make this piece what it is, a poem—as Lowell would say later about Berryman's *Dream Songs*—"more tearful and funny than we can easily bear." The place is Maine, and Lowell spends the poem's first half in playful overview of the town that has just lost its "summer millionaire, / who seemed to leap from an L.L. Bean / catalogue." But the humor turns quickly to something more personally chilling.

One dark night,
My Tudor Ford climbed the hill's skull;
I watched for love-cars. Lights turned down,
they lay together, hull to hull,
where the graveyard shelves on the town. . . .
My mind's not right.

A car radio bleats,
"Love, O careless Love. . . . " I hear
my ill-spirit sob in each blood cell,
as if my hand were at its throat. . . .
I myself am hell;
nobody's here—

It might be impossible not to follow this musically, its rush at once urgent and languid, and not be reminded of Pound's up-from-schoolmarmish pronouncement to make poems in the musical phrase not the metronome's, though our sound has moved inward to silence and its empty spaces, less dependent on an American street cadence, that public sound Williams relished. The fragility of Graham's poem or Lowell's seems heartbreakingly clear partly because we watch the lines themselves pause and drop. Paul Klee again: "Art: that thing which is never expressed purely as result." Through line we watch the thing unfold as something put together, the takes and double takes, the way actual thought is made. Not so crucial, then, the big-bang summary ending, the I-have-wasted-my-life part. Brooks and Warren's old breakdown between the sentence's *sense* and the line's *attention* takes on a stranger meaning in much of contemporary verse, our love of the broken and the piecemeal, our *inattention* to—or loss of faith in—the grand overview. When one thinks in lines, it's a curious kind of dismemberment, the part at least equally treasured as the whole.

Which is a thing the hand knows down to its smallest muscle and bone in a world where line has always been visual and made bit by bit. In the *Chieh Tzu Yüän Hua Chuan* or *The Mustard Seed Garden Manual of Painting*, a book of ancient origin but assembled in China around 1700, the line *means* in a rich confetti of ways from its simple run of here to there, ink to paper, to nothing less than linking two sides of the universe, all that is *yang*—or light—in the line against all that is *yin*—or dark—repeated endlessly in the paper's pale weave, a surprising inversion. As with the poetic line, one feels weight in the movement, but this time it's the brush, its *tun*, all verb as it dots and flicks and moves forward "sweeping, turning, plunging, thinning out." And to study a painting—or, I'd add, a poem—is to feel through line the press and lift of thought *as it happens*, forget that such a moment took place in the past. Lowell's sorrow in "Skunk Hour" is suggested by an abrupt enjambment carried over from his earlier verse or in the disquieting ellipsis, that weighted place at the end of a line that floats meaning into something one dare not say. Both moves suggest the unfinished, the still-living thing.

How deeply all this connects to the body is the real test, brush-marks themselves spoken of in the *Manual* as "muscles," meaning the "short, sinewy strokes" while "bones" are "the longer and firm ones," flesh itself "the rise and fall of the rhythm of their forms and connecting strokes." Most vital is the *ch'i*, the spirit on which life depends, the thing that probably took the top of Dickinson's head right off if we believe her irresistible remark on what a good poem might do if left to its own and often dangerous devices.

∽

Such danger, if we refigure just right, might bring us to more recent revolutions. Black Mountain College then. Go by way of the ch'i, the brush held and lowered as the spirit—the breath—runs through the body, taking us back to the said thing, the heard thing, all the resources of the page toward that. But to hear Charles Olson, so gritty and urgent, as he begins his extraordinary essay "Projective Verse," is to hear—has anyone ever said this out loud?—writing that sounds like a bad translation of something quite brilliant. "Verse now, 1950, if it is to go ahead, if it is to be of essential use, I take it, catch up and put into itself certain laws and possibilities of breathing of the man who writes as well as of his listeners. . . ."

How the line actually works into these laws and possibilities turns out to be the tricky thing, but first there's a larger theory, one that would shape a generation of poets, Levertov and Creeley among them and so many coming after, Olson's "COMPOSITION BY FIELD," the phrase virtually shouted through his weird habit of running favorite dictums in capital letters, his "FORM IS NEVER MORE THAN AN EXTEN-SION OF CONTENT," for instance, a subset of the theory or any other hot-to-the-touch, kinetic plea—"ONE PERCEPTION MUST IMMEDIATELY AND DIRECTLY LEAD TO A FURTHER PERCEPTION" or "MOVE INSTANTER, ON ANOTHER!" Eventually his thoughts on line are amplified too, how-beit in snaggly bits.

> And the line comes (I swear it) from the breath, from the breathing of the man who writes, at the moment he writes, and thus is, it is here that, the daily work, the WORK, gets in.

Or this:

> Let me put it baldly. "The two halves are: the HEAD by way of the EAR, to the SYLLABLE. The HEART by way of the BREATH, to the LINE . . . surprise, it is the LINE that's the baby that gets, as the poem is getting made, the attention, the control that is right here, in the line, that the shaping takes place, each moment of the going."

"Each moment of the going . . ." Again, that painterly weight on the part, not the whole, but here it's crucial to Olson's passion for the end-line pause because line *is* so unlike the sentence, whose deft flow moves the paragraph to closure with little need for more than ordinary punctuation to soften, then turn it. Olson's instructions are specific: "If a contemporary poet leaves a space as long as a phrase before it, that space is to be held, by the breath, an equal length of time . . . he [*sic*] means that time to pass that it takes the eye—that hair of time suspended—to pick up the next line." In spirit, Olson's remark could be close to what Roethke liked to say, quoting Lawrence, that "it all depends on the pause, the natural pause." Or close to any number of poets who have stressed silence as an equal presence to what is voiced. Still, the one phrase buried here, set apart by its mute dashes—"that hair of time suspended"—is *synapse* for whatever leap, all things unsayable coming up in the pause. There's no other place in our literary forms where one can speak then take back—for an instant—what was said. Nowhere but poetry, where such uncertainty is encouraged, in fact worked architecturally into the very shape of things, line into room, room opening to another by angle and cross angle, the actual process of human understanding and its limits so visible.

It wasn't strictly rhetorical to Olson or dreamily a matter of program music. The matter of line was preliterate for him, even genetic, a poetic DNA that shapes spirit, rising as breath, in turn, to shape the original poem. Each utterance has lasting weight in such a view, but "to see the word for what it is, one needs the line." That's Charles Simic again, though Olson might have added, in spite of its seeming paradox, that one needs to see where the line ends, where its words stop. Or perhaps all of this, at best, is illusion and there are no lines, as Nicolaides claims in his still popular drawing manual from the 1930s. There is only the place "where the figure ceases." So in poetry, even in our sense of line, one of the smallest mechanics of the genre, we're reminded continually of that inevitable darkness into which all things vanish.

〰

When I lived in Maine, we liked to drive randomly, taking roads which themselves spidered off to smaller roads, passing meadows and creekbeds and every wild green expanse. One road was our favorite. We followed it north, oak and maple and ash thickening on either side, until there was no road. Even on the map the thin line staggered, then violently broke into nothing. I would track it on paper, stare down at the thing. But I loved more going into that nowhere. Where the road simply stopped, we'd sit in our old Volkswagen, glad and grief-stricken at once, everything human swallowed up by trees on three sides, the vast tangle before us so many miles and thousands of lifetimes deep. "Some roads end abruptly in the woods," I wrote later, haunted by the place or the line. But that poem—I never finished it.

Decoys

I think now it was the getting there that kept me going back, something one might dream against too many nights of not dreaming. It was cutting *mauka* on the Pali around 7 A.M., up the ancient Koolau Range, high enough for cloud forest, northeast toward windward Oahu, southeast at Kailua, past Waimanalo, the blaze of sea always at my left. Still, the islands surprised me every time, Rabbit Island and its smaller neighbor, the one I'd come for, Kaohikaipu, risen up in some prehistoric firestorm, now idle, a flat thing broken off, seemingly forgotten a half mile out. Or I liked most my wheels on gravel, turning sharply into the lot at Sea Life Park early, before it opened, the plain details of my watch: showing my Hawaii Audubon badge, taking up my weapons and instruments—beach umbrella, binoculars, bird book, thermos of ice and sandwich, my old Purdue Women's Basketball cap. Then the walk to the office, working open the battered locker to find again the small necessities I shared with other volunteers—lawn chair and spotting scope, the data book I would add to, scribbling my observations every quarter hour, any live albatross among the decoys on Kaohikaipu be they preening or sleeping or pacing about, all signs that the birds might come back, might have a thought to nest there after centuries and thus be safe. Because they weren't safe in those other places, flat expanses they chose on Oahu, always airfields, military or commercial. Thus this new plan concocted by the state and by Audubon that might draw them down to the perfect site to mate and raise their young even if it took decoys to do it, a slew of fake happy albatross as bait, as *wow-that-could-be-us*.

Really, it wasn't difficult getting there week after week, nor the climb to the site we were given at the park. Past dolphins performing their antics for no one, past the corny two-masted schooner, I reached the edge, the last outcropping before the plunge to the highway where, just beyond, the ocean lay heaving and shining. An *overlook*. To look over and out to sea, to the island where I had promised to look. So I made camp for the morning in rain or in light, set my scope on the spidery tripod and pulled out from the distant sweep of beauty its deliberate particulars, suddenly looming, up close. Certain rare moments, I could put my eye on an albatross eye, or perhaps I imagined that, one or two turned in my direction, those bodies landing awkwardly, walking the island curious about the decoys, stretching. Then they stood still.

They stood still and if I first noticed them a moment *after* that moment, my troubles began. Harder to figure which might be which, a live albatross simply at rest or, no, just a wooden decoy. I'd watch carefully for movement, but some I came upon were sleeping; it would be many minutes before they stirred, their dreams—if albatross drift through such things—taking them a great distance. It might seem easy enough to distinguish, the decoys larger, clearer in their markings, some whose pretense was obvious like those passionately paired in a ritualistic mating dance, beaks raised for mooing and clicking and rattling love calls, all neatly supplied by way of the solar-powered CD player set up nearby. But the occasional, honest-to-god albatross stock still, oblivious or dozing, or the single decoys scattered about, these I studied, stared down: which were real and which were art?

Ancient question, enriching, no, plaguing us since the dim start of human life, the cave drawings in the Dordogne, for instance, showing a single figure with its antlered headdress to purposes we imagine dark with grievance. Past that, we imagine their function, a decoy to draw the beast out, enchant it into reach and certain death by its own faint recognition, whatever real creature in the undergrowth, vaguely aware—*this thing like me*. Artifice, art itself then, against the grim knock of hunger, the hunter's urgent wish to survive the next season and the next. So we make brutal drama of the past, whirl backward then forward. So I watched those decoys, unlikely mute figures on an island two thousand miles from any continent, watched them exact their fabled deception to summon out of air their real counterparts, the exotic albatross, birds that considered and came closer, this time, not for death.

Too many contradictions—the killing habit of decoys but now a lure for safety's sake, actual untidy creatures against so many well-mannered fakes, life against art or from art, or to art. Because I have trouble with these distinctions, I have trouble with poetry, wanting the real life behind its ordering but wanting too its zoom-lens habit of enlarging certain moments of discovery, freezing them as good painting does, good sculpture does. All art is a kind of exaggeration, of course, itself and analogy both; there is, even in the smallest poem, this wish for more. It might be image or pace or a shift of diction; something *suggests*. The diagnostic feature, Roger Tory Peterson wrote in his preface to the 1939 edition of his *Field Guide to the Birds*, was, after all, merely "a simplification," a "boiling down," a matter of impression and pattern rather than anatomical difference and measurement. His illustrations overplaying such things would set a new course for ornithology. For decoy making, an art practiced since prehistory, it was always the obvious tactic, crucial to the art, wrote carver and collector Joel Barber long after Peterson's breakthrough. The point is to be "symbolic rather than naturalistic," to aim for "a quiet, perfect buoy of species," things best understood at a distance.

My own distance, as I focused on the decoys, gradually taught me to see their white bodies too white against the real ones. And their black wings, perfectly etched, everything about them more orderly and grander than the real albatross, those wind- and water-beaten creatures, bedraggled, only half curious as if the former, as lure, were simply a sea-weary vision of extravagance and romance—a Club Med of phony albatross coupling, the CD's taped calls booming around them. Finally there comes a point in the drama when actual birds meet the pretend ones, some moment when the veil of enchantment lifts. To poems, sooner or later, one brings one's real life.

Given: the complicated though undramatic commonplace of most days and weeks and years. What to do then with Whitman's manic bravado, say, his very unquiet but "perfect buoy of species" in "Song of Myself," its dizzying versions of self by way of Cecil B. DeMille, every stranger from convict to surgeon to stevedore imagined, blown up, bigger than life. He had reasons, of course, crazy for the grand overview. He lived in cities after all—New York, Philadelphia, Washington—and walked them daily, keeping notes, his eye a camera's eye, that new invention he thought so ingenious. So often he was defining, generalizing—American Youth or American Motherhood, the American Solider Like No Other, American Big Thing or Small Thing, Americans abstracted to all generosity and quick, the best of human impulse, no longer the old world, England, or any other place, an enlargement of spirit dreamt for his countrymen and for himself.

Not such an original notion, with the country so young, to tout and embellish. It was Emerson's too and even Thoreau's, though one's grateful for a certain crankiness in *Walden*, an unexpected stay against excess. On and on goes the oddly crowded solitude of Whitman's plea to be all and everyone, to unloose the doors from their jambs, to hear every animal, every windblown bit of vegetation, all human cries as a god might hear the world were it possible even to imagine such omniscience. He can't get to the end of it, or in getting near the end—here in one of the final sections—he cannot stop though he brilliantly stages a hesitation in which to think, and think again.

> There is that in me—I do not know what it is—but I know it
> is in me.

> Wrench'd and sweaty—calm and cool then my body
> becomes,
> I sleep—I sleep long.

> I do not know it—it is without name—it is a word unsaid,
> It is not in any dictionary, utterance, symbol.

> Something it swings on more than the earth I swing on,
> To it the creation is the friend whose embracing awakes me.

> Perhaps I might tell more. Outlines! I plead for my brothers
> and sisters.

> Do you see O my brothers and sisters?
> It is not chaos or death—it is form, union, plan—it is eternal
> life—it is Happiness.

It's the "Happiness" here that surprises, coming as it does after "eternal life," a trigger if there ever was one in that century for the conventional pieties to let go their tedious beleaguer. Instead, we get happiness as the great find, capitalized in case there was doubt, delivered out of the vast goodness of the poem, its endurance and burst, its will to live for some eighty pages if we consider the first edition. *A simplification*, wrote Peterson, intent as he was on making hawks and warblers in broad strokes, accessible as cartoon to lure us into woods and into accurate—for the first time widely possible— observation. But often I feel impatient with Whitman's rushed images in spite of their startling detail, impatient with their caricature, thinking nineteenth-century America surely more than a medley of simultaneous stills, each figure caught in its definitive gesture of trade or gender, courage or longing, each an emblem, a bit of a decoy, to bring down—what? I'm not good at this, I think then, caught between the charm of his energy and his exhausting takes and retakes.

⁓

I wasn't only *watching* decoys. When Sea Life Park opened those mornings, I became, unwittingly as dolphin or seal, one of the attractions myself, the place flooded with tourists, school groups, an occasional local person, usually with out-of-state houseguests in tow. I wasn't as picturesque as a sea lion or as good-natured. My one advantage: I spoke when spoken to. Between my quarter-hour scans and data jottings, I was easy prey, merely reading or writing or mostly dreaming off somewhere. School groups would stop, the teacher in command—always that loud, earnest enunciation—leaning close to ask her predictable question. And I'd say exactly what I was supposed to say: no, not whales but albatross whose nests were at risk on Oahu, liking as they did flat, barren places in the sun, like runways, not a happy choice given the air traffic on the island. Thus treeless Kaohikaipu—I'd let them take turns at the scope—and now decoys there, set out to lure down the albatross, to announce the place as a natal site. And always the teacher would turn to her bored and distracted charges. See children, she'd say. Here is a real scientist doing real scientist things, writing in this little notebook—she'd grab and hoist it for all to see. I thought about my fate then, watching decoys on an island from an island, myself no less a decoy, a scientist decoy fooling kids pretending themselves to be interested while they mainly thought *when's lunch?* or *all right! ten o'clock and we're not in math class!* But I liked the feel of it, those moments I was species, *scientist*, my scientist things in hand—island charts, data book, a pen with its black rainproof ink that might, maybe, add one tiny half-bit to the tireless march toward understanding life on this planet. True to my decoydom, I looked straight at her, nodding, and never admitted otherwise.

I'm not so certain about poetry though. Because I am one of those—that's clear—who can't help, in the first half-second, naïvely thinking that the "I" in the poem must be the writer's, at least in the personal lyric, our predominant form for years now, this in spite of the fact that when talking about any piece, I refer, as is the custom these days, to "the speaker," a useful distancing agent, regardless. Like any art, poetry begins and ends a made thing, idle or urgent; it is separate from its creator. It is, it is, I tell myself and believe myself, sensing that curious truth each time I write, working toward a poem and it finds me instead. Why, then, my nearly stricken feeling when once, after a young woman's poem about a toddler drowning—the "speaker's" toddler—was discussed in workshop, the author admitted nonchalantly to her consoling classmates—several of them older than she, with children themselves, thus easily wounded by the poem's grief—that she had no child; it was all made up; don't worry about it, no one died at all.

The resulting rage in that room was palpable. I understood it well enough even as I said what is routinely said, that a poet has a right to explore anything, that the emotional connection to the subject matter, and thus her control of tone, was real if indeed the actual story in the poem was not. Something made the piece work, if by *work* one may say it moved a roomful of people by its authenticity. The young, inexperienced writer nevertheless managed this authority and thus their anger, I suppose: they'd been *had*, their own sympathy for nothing, their classmate appropriating a thing about which, they were sure now, she never had a clue.

It wasn't manipulation exactly, at least not as melodrama demands it, strong feeling out of nowhere we're expected, on cue, to share. The poet in fact had been relatively careful in her imagery to build a convincing crisis. Still, I've never seen before or since such outrage in a classroom. I turn these things over and think this would never bother a novelist. But poetry isn't fiction. For good or ill, our immediate assumptions about these two genres differ, though dream can and does take the poem into regions way past fact, and mere commentary *upon* or mere rendering of *what actually happened* almost always holds it back.

Of course, many subjects are used remotely, metaphorically really, to work out whatever personal confession, angelic or demonic. There's Whitman, for one, whose longing in *Memoranda*, his notes on visits to Civil War hospitals, led him to write almost amorously of death embracing the young soldiers, though he was never one to deny himself the pleasure of plain speaking. Poets find themselves writing about gardens or weather or whatever ordinary thing because direct love is forbidden or direct grief or certain angers. Or not forbidden as much as unspeakable somehow, as if blatantly giving words to a thing might bury it or cheapen it, at least change it. Thus the roundabout of some very bad poems, and some very good ones too, Plath's bee sequence for instance, which takes on marital separation at its lowest real-life ebb and nothing short of transformation at its highest. Only through inference does that first level even come clear. My student's link to sorrow was genuine enough though perhaps not the specific tragedy she put on paper.

Empathy, in whatever form, is one of the gifts, indeed one of the ambitions of art, the great *other* out there no longer distant but *in here*, a point few would dismiss entirely. Meanwhile, there's probably a very thin line between empathy and appropriation, though it's likely impossible to make any fair, useable distinction. Poem by poem, it becomes a matter of tact and balance; no rule of logic, no formula helps. In the name of poetic truth, all manner of liberties must be taken, so Aristotle first argued in his *Poetics*, drawing out differences between history and poetry, the former describing something that *was*, against the latter's concern with what might, in its place, *be possible*. Which proves at least the question is old enough never to be answered or endlessly answered. The lived moment or the imagined one. The lived moment *and* the imagined one. Still, it occurs to me that the highest praise I find myself giving a piece of writing, particularly one in first person, is to say simply: I forgot I was reading. Which is to say, I forgot this was art. My initial old-fashioned assumption that the poet *is* the speaker in such a piece must be part of this. We're witness, then, to a life lived. Good poems make one believe that, regardless of fact.

A number of poets, however, quite obviously speak in voices not their own. This ventriloquist's impulse hardens to near genre with the so-called "persona poem," a valued form of the dramatic lyric. Randall Jarrell comes to mind with his flat, proselike poems from a woman's point of view, a cross-dressing literary feat that seems oddly riskier now than when he wrote them in the 1950s and early 1960s. They're uneven; some survive better than others the translation from his historical moment to ours, against the current notion of what is plausible when characterizing a thing so unfathomable as the other gender. The best of them, I think, is "The Lost Children" from his 1965 collection, his last, *The Lost World*, the speaker an older woman thinking of her daughters, one living and one dead, who come back to her via photographs when her one remaining child, now grown, visits with her husband who "enjoys . . . / and makes fun" of the pictures. To the mother, caught quick by the reality of the past—and here's Jarrell's originality at work—it's less a matter of wound than of astonishment to stare at the album, the girls with pet duck and tin lunchbox, matching hats, sand castles. "I look at them," the mother thinks, "and all the old sure knowledge / Floods over me."

I keep saying inside: "I *did* know those children.
I braided those braids. I was driving the car
The day that she stepped in the can of grease
We were taking to the butcher for our ration points.
I know those children. I know all about them.
Where are they?"

I stare at her and try to see some sign
Of the child she was. I can't believe there isn't any.
I tell her foolishly, pointing to the picture,
That I keep wondering where she is.
She tells me, "Here I am."
                                    Yes, and the other
Isn't dead, but has everlasting life . . .

The girl from next door, the borrowed child,
Said to me the other day, "You like children so much,
Don't you want to have some of your own?"
I couldn't believe that she could say it.
I thought: "Surely you can look at me and see them."

Lost children maybe, but here the mother is also quite alone; the
living daughter, she feels, has "discarded" her, pain distanced early in
the poem by second-, third-person shifts—"She argues with you, or
ignores you / Or is kind to you. She who begged to follow you /
Anywhere, just so long as it was you / . . . she makes few demands:
you are grateful for the few." The slow but inevitable success of this
piece might be more a matter of what Jarrell shared with its presumed
speaker and the speaker's child—his growing up and away from his
own mother and, later, step-parenthood, which he cherished—rather
than what he couldn't share, though he carries off well what it's like
to bear a child, "to know it before it's born; / to see at last it's a boy or
a girl, and perfect / . . . to watch it / Nurse at your breast, till you

almost know it / Better than you know yourself—better than it knows itself." It's Jarrell's genius not to strain or embellish what he hasn't lived himself.

Another piece in the same collection, "Next Day," is less convincing to me although much is remarkable about the poem including the beginning, deadpan play of language that could only happen in a supermarket—"Moving from Cheer to Joy, from Joy to All, I take a box / And add it to my wild rice, my Cornish game hens." The speaker of these lines is caught in the former speaker's same dislocation of age and gender. The usual contexts of identity and success are unraveling, at center a woman equally alone though here the catalyst is not a daughter but a stranger, the grocery boy carrying sacks to her car. And the emotional result is vastly different.

> When I was young and miserable and pretty
> And poor, I'd wish
> What all girls wish: to have a husband,
> A house and children. Now that I'm old, my wish
> Is womanish:
> That the boy putting groceries in my car
>
> See me. It bewilders me he doesn't see me.
> For so many years
> I was good enough to eat: the world looked at me
> And its mouth watered.

That this ordinary incident launches a fevered meditation on love and power lost, on inevitable physical diminishment and death is, I suppose, credible. My unease with this piece comes not because grocery boys never warrant this torrent of doubt and self-hatred, nor certainly not because these fears among women are impossible. It's that the terms of discovery in the poem follow so predictably, the speaker so near to type, embarrassingly close to a rather wistful male version of women as beings who see themselves only in the context of their relationship to men, to a beauty designed to attract them. Of course such a figure laments her failing powers as temptress. Of course she experiences the death of her friend not by mourning her but as precursor to her own eventual decay: "My friend's cold made-up face, granite among its flowers, / Her undressed, operated-on, dressed body / Were my face and body." We know all things already; it's the decimal rounded out to its whole number; she's every woman if we buy cliché.

And we must buy it in part because clichés are true—thus their power—as decoys are true. They approximate and render the species, which every poem must, to be universal. But good poems also give us what is individual, each particular human strangeness; that part grants life. There was a French thinker in natural history around 1750, George-Louis Buffon, who stoutly, to much ridicule, defended his view of organization against Linnaeus's more lasting classification of animals, claiming that large grouping—species-making—was, at best, a convenient coinage of the human mind. "In fact only individuals exist in Nature," he insisted. "The more one multiplies sub-divisions among objects in Natural History, the closer one comes to reality."

At Sea Life Park in the duration of my watch, I saw tourist after tourist, American or Japanese, lined up with families, even grandma against the shimmering blue-washed backdrop. They grinned for eternity briefly but long enough for the daughter or uncle at the tripod to set the timer and run to join the line. I was always hearing the camera's whirr, its blip blip blip and the emphatic final click. In that fierce light, some were squinting more than smiling. But I always longed for one of them to let loose with an uncalculated face to break the staged moment of family harmony or honeymoon bliss or the grimly happy this-is-costing-me-plenty look of so many retired couples. I wished for mischief, a second frozen for the album that didn't follow the script. It amazes me I never saw it though each time, right after, I noticed something—everyone easier, the self-consciousness passed like the fear of a hurricane, real joking or annoyance again, regular breathing. Or I dreamt these small distinctions because I was sometimes idle, or the place too beautiful.

∼

And dream, what creature is that? The one that, frozen and fixed but nevertheless like pain or desire, calls out to us from its own island? Or is it that thing, in us or through us, which answers? Sometime in the seventh century, the first person who would write a lyric poem in English had a dream, was told in the dream—by man or angel, it isn't entirely clear—to write that poem. The sleeper himself, Caedmon, had been unwilling, refusing just that evening to take his turn at the harp when the storytelling and singing began after the feast, feeling he had no talent for it, was stupid, had nothing to tell let alone sing. Returning to the stable where he slept with the animals he cared for, he lay down and dreamt the wonderfully matter-of-fact conversation rendered by Bede in 731.

> There stood by him in a dream a man, who saluted and greeted
> him, calling him by name: Caedmon, sing me something. Then
> he answered and said: I know not how to sing. I therefore from
> the beer-ship went out, departed, because I naught to sing know.
> Again he who spoke to him said: But you shall sing to me. And
> Caedmon said: What? What shall I sing? Said he: Sing me the
> beginning of the creatures.

Once convinced, Caedmon did begin to sing, waking to recall every word about this *middangeard* or "middle-earth" of ours, heaven-created *to hrofe*, "as roof," that close. Or so he inventively describes in the only poem coming down to us. But Caedmon apparently never stopped making more words until his happy death, retelling in verse countless scriptural events, hymns of praise really though nothing seems to match Bede's regard for Caedmon himself or for the poet's astonishment to the end that such things came through him.

I like this story too much, its forward momentum against the want and warfare of Caedmon's age, not a great deal in that time to be glad for. I like the poet's self-effacement and his surprise that he suddenly understood these things, songs or poems, and how to make them with or without dreaming, a gift that extended, Bede wrote, to knowing the exact night he would die and how to manage it, a clear premonition in spite of apparent good health and his companions' disbelief. I forgive even the innocent pitch of Bede's telling, the romantic gloss that makes it a kind of dream about a dream so we find ourselves in some weird complexity of half-wild goodness. What part of Caedmon's story or his poem is myth and what part fact *I can't know*, as my nephew said over and over before he started school and more grave than he would ever be again, answering the silly questions I put to him.

This is, I think, some of the pleasure good dreams offer us, this *not knowing*, even while it's half the dark in any nightmare. Best is the notion that our poetry began this way, reluctantly, a gift to someone who doubted that gift. First doubt, then curiosity takes over; then larger, something out of the great world, and stranger. This profound *otherness* in poems, down to their origin, might well be the element that makes them poems at all and not autobiography or merely therapy, a means to an end. But that intricate leap, more patience than leap perhaps—how to manage it? How to get past the bare facts of a life to call down genuine broad connection without too much of Peterson's "boiling down" or "simplification," without exaggeration or perhaps just enough to signal those of us paused, as any reader is, at a distance.

So I am watchful, thinking how the Irish poet Eavan Boland does it, say, in her poem "Anna Liffey," working half-hesitation against authority in a long meditative sweep through concentric matters of self, family, nation. On the face of it is Caedmon's reluctance again, this time the speaker stopped alone to see herself merely—and eternally—as "a woman in a doorway," the phrase coming again and again, a recurrence of image that might appear amplified in dreams, though here its ordinary shine grounds and opens. Because there are maps to take us there, she presents their large specifics—that the Liffey is a river named for a woman, that one sees black peat and ling heather, swans, herons, "the smudged air and bridges of Dublin" which the river itself runs through, its water a "shiftless and glittering / re-telling of a city." Past that, this movement is a kind of spell; her brief fragmented lines carry us—where, into what?

There's personal history in the poem, children called home at dusk, a woman aging and the body knowing a new kind of longing; then cold weather, rainy weather, a brick house, a porch light. Against that, a city and a country with its violent history and its myth—"Make of a nation what you will," she writes, "Make of the past / What you can." The poem moves in symphonic fashion, its themes musical threads woven and rewoven until there is distance between speaker and what has been spoken of, where the poet can do the impossible and show herself credibly as *woman*, as "figure in a poem." Here is species then, a luminous moment of coherence. Because, as Boland tells it, "In the end / It will not matter / That I am a woman. / The body is a source. Nothing more / . . . Consider rivers," she says,

> They are always en route to
> Their own nothingness. From the first moment
> They are going home. And so
> When language cannot do it for us,
> Cannot make us know love will not diminish us,

There are these phrases
Of the ocean
to console us.
Particular and unafraid of their completion.
In the end
Everything that burdened and distinguished me
Will be lost in this:
I was a voice.

A voice, the poet says, awake now like Caedmon and yet completely unlike him, the world given way to this knowledge beyond love into the hard and endless form of things.

Certainly a poem like Boland's with its elegiac pace and primal imagery ties us to the history not only of place but of sorrow, an impulse in poetry from the first. When I knew I'd be watching albatross in the months ahead, I searched the elephant folios in the library to find the first and probably last word on that species via Coleridge, his *Rime of the Ancient Mariner*, which started out humbly enough, a brief verse-tale-to-be for a popular magazine based vaguely on the dream of a neighbor and written to fund a walking tour, both the writing and walking a joint venture of Wordsworth and himself. But early on Wordsworth got bored and Coleridge too passionate, the former dropping out and the poem no longer a quick scam but a monster only Coleridge could love.

I wanted the 1875 edition with the giant full-scale Doré illustrations, thirty-eight woodcuts that Coleridge, dying some forty years earlier, never saw. I was in the deep shade of too many books and opened the mammoth library copy to the stilled immediate violence of the poem: the companion ghost ship, manned by death herself; then the infamous albatross, first above the frozen seas as luck itself boding a southern wind, next fed by the sorry crew to keep that good omen, later shot by the speaker of the tale out of sport or malice or both—the poet never says—the slip of arrow white against thousands of inked lines that make blackest night. Every page is such, set by Doré past Coleridge into a darkness only the Victorians understood without self-consciousness, their genius for disaster inevitably linked to their genius for order. Several engravings show the poor albatross limp, nearly as large as the killer and hung around his neck but it was the lifeless bodies of the crew that stopped me, each face glassy-eyed, staring inward. There are those who can follow such a look, but I could not.

It was only "a poet's reverie." Or so Coleridge felt called upon to explain, adding these words as subtitle in all editions after its run in the first version of *Lyrical Ballads* co-authored with Wordsworth, though the phrase annoyed many, including Charles Lamb who thought it not redundant but an insincere disclaimer about a poem whose virtue lay less in what was imagined than in what was real. The imagined? "All the miraculous part of it," said Lamb. Which left the real—those "feelings of the man under the operation of such scenery." Then going on to argue against those who wanted more detail in the mariner, a past life for him, personal minutiae, Lamb underscored one of the poem's psychological truths, that "such trials . . . overwhelm and bury all individuality or memory of what (a person) was." Transformation then, through poetic voice, means a different sort of *being* one hears, a stranger, even as one writes it down, or reads it.

In fact, Coleridge's mariner is condemned to relive this trial over and over for anyone who will half-listen, the poor wedding guest, for instance, collared on his way to the festivities, held back by this story in the moment that begins the piece. The *anyone who will listen* includes us, I suppose, two centuries later, all part of the vast, even surreal hopelessness of the poem to go on and on, as art goes on. Nevertheless, the mariner is a survivor, unaccountably so, left to speak of the awful journey though he must walk the earth to do so, more abstracted, less personal by the minute though more human, one of

Plato's eternal forms, the shape of something—pure spirit or idea—beyond the thing itself. Those months in Hawaii, I sometimes watched a real albatross standing next to its decoy, exactly as the wedding guest stood, as we might stand, at the start of the poem. The bird seemed puzzled, even frightened. In a few moments though, he relaxed, and began to preen this odd creature he recognized.

WILLIAMS AND THE BOMB

It was cool for July, that day in Seattle, midcentury almost. I close my eyes to imagine it: William Carlos Williams delivering his bold address, "Poetry as a Field of Action," at the University of Washington, hoping to shock American poetry into what was then hailed with generally optimistic feeling as the Atomic Age. This isn't pure imagination. We have the year—1948—and, of course, the speech itself. We have the poet's astounding, even outrageous connections, forcing that most dramatic nub of nuclear power—the A-bomb—into a daring metaphor for thought itself. "One great thing about the bomb," he told them, "is the awakened sense it gives us that catastrophic (but why?) alterations are also possible in the human *mind*, in art, in the arts."

From here, Williams spun down to a more familiar focus: his ways and rationalizations for continual experimentation in American verse. He lingered over his variable foot, which took his thirst for change deep as structure then out into the street where one could hear the cadence, real people with their real and tender and wiseacre speech, *American* speech, from which to write. Yet in his brief remarks about the bomb, something much more potent stirred. Like many Americans in the late 1940s, he hovered between the greatest hope and fear before this powerful turn in science, but as a poet, Williams saw in the nightmare the glow of creativity itself. "We are too cowed by our fear to realize it fully," he added, "but it is possible." If the dark center of energy itself could alter, perhaps the furious shifting would force poetry to an intensity new to the world. "This isn't optimism," he argued, "it is chemistry; or better, physics."

It's hard to think straight—that is, kindly—about such remarks. Which is to say after the H-bomb, the Cold War, after the massive threat of the bomb, which forced a whole generation to grow up worried sick or just plain worried about *what if* and *if so, will the family's fallout shelter be enough?* That is, if your family had such a shelter with its gleaming bottles of water, canned tuna and peas, state-of-the-art air-filter vent. Mine didn't. All that aside, I'm trying to imagine that day, that peculiar moment in time. Because behind Williams's seeming and rather horrific bravado as he pushed his metaphor that July afternoon, stood an idea he had long considered: that in physics, poetry had found its rambunctious, combustible twin.

A little history then that, zygotelike, shows this clear connection. In the early years of the century, young physicists studying at Göttingen—J. Robert Oppenheimer, for one, Werner Heisenberg, for another—had entered a world where past knowledge, familiar and logical ways of doing things, simply no longer carried weight. At the same time, as though thought really lives outside the head as Plato might have it, hovering there so that ideas can occur to many not just to one, it was the imagists growing equally impatient with *their* givens—conventional poetic shape and sound and substance— getting bold enough for a manifesto. Thus *Poetry* emerged, Anderson and Heap's *Little Review*, Kreymborg's *Others*, all seeking ways to vitalize the poem itself. But the artery between physics and poetry lay deeper, and, more than most of his contemporaries, Williams, as much from temperament as from education, seemed to know why.

As the century turned, atomic science, with its remarkably precise instruments, had crept quietly into being to attract a curious sort of follower. Like other branches of science, physics was slowly growing, as Whitehead has pointed out, "anti-rational" in the sense that it had become, given its finely wrought new tools, far more than mere "organized common sense" concerning natural phenomena that anyone could make out by sight alone. The world pursued by these new scientists where the atom held tight to its secret was minute, utterly private, but it was something more: absolutely theoretical. No one in those early decades had any genuine notion about worldly use for nuclear fission. To harness such power? Was that a joke? A serious thought? Until the fierce military-backed effort of World War II with its assembly of the first bomb, *applied* atomic science seemed a contradiction in terms. In the first years, those drawn to such pure research were working like monks perhaps, apolitical and content to be isolated behind the high imagination of mathematics and the dazzle of exotic instruments, in the tight camaraderie not of national interest but of scientific zeal. And Williams? This is where his fascination must have been at least partly temperamental. For him, such isolation seemed to be familiar, even comfortable. "The great world," he remarked years later, "never much interested me (except at the back of my head) since its effects from what I observed were so disastrously trivial." With half of his life-energies sunk into medicine, that so applied of sciences, Williams might have seen in physics something close to what he wanted in poetry: a technical means to measure and record "some secret twist . . . of the underground stream," that "glimpse of something time to time" underlying the common chaos of the everyday overwhelming him as a physician.

The shared approach of physics and poetry showed itself throughout Williams's development as a writer. In his collection of essays and prose pieces *The Embodiment of Knowledge*, dashed off in part between patients in the years 1928 to 1930, he admitted to troubling contradictions in his view of science but claimed at last its usefulness in understanding the "effect of speed" in poems "or the intensities involved especially with reference to the rhythm that affects words as it does sand or whatever else is in motion." How deep a connection was he making? "It can be explained," he wrote, "by physics, and not grammar."

By the time of these remarks, we know he had absorbed the new physics enough to affect the future of his own verse line. In 1926 he had read an important collection of lectures given by C. P. Steinmetz on relativity and carried on lengthy discussions about them with John Roidan, the young engineer who had lent him the book. In the same year, Roidan gave him Whitehead's *Science and the Modern World;* Williams not only urged his wife to read it, he inscribed the flyleaf, clearly smitten: "A milestone in my career, should I have the force and imagination to go on with my work." The structural impact of relativity and quantum mechanics on Williams's notion of the variable foot—as critics such as Mike Weaver have pointed out—is old news, beyond question. But the nuclear presence made deeper inroads in Williams's imagination. First finding in it a formal technique and a philosophy to underpin it, he came finally to face it in a bold conceptual sense, not simply as *idea* but in its incarnation as weapon, as bomb, the thing itself, which is to say, as *image*. That such an image can scare us to death—that matters, I think. And that it scared Williams—from this fact, perhaps, comes its most lasting power, especially as time moves us closer to its dark possibilities.

The possibilities were not always evident, however, and the poet's shift from awe to alarm was a gradual stop-start, backward-forward affair. The Williams of those early years—the 1920s through the 1940s, years when scientific structure made its crossover into his idea of line and rhythm—was not the Williams of the 1950s, after the first detonation of the hydrogen bomb. Not that the poet was unusual in his growing doubts and dread. His counterparts in the sciences exploded in concern about the new threat; we have, for instance, the Atomic Scientists of Chicago organizing lectures and letter-writing campaigns and publishing their *Bulletin* to work for control of the arms race. In Williams, such an awakening, far more subtle, can be seen by tracing his fascination with nuclear imagery from the early infatuation in *Paterson* to his chilling, thoughtful handling in the much later poem "Asphodel, that Greeny Flower." In the process, we're deep into a thing immensely private and hard to talk about, how the imagination itself develops, the genuine mystery of that. But something enormously public, historic even and far more urgent, echoes here: how the twentieth-century mind comes alert to its own recklessness. Or *if* it does. And either way, *what then.*

～

At the start it was simple, I think: Williams sitting down like a child before his first eclipse, the everyday world fallen into taboo, the impossible, possible. Say, an ordinary blue and white day abruptly darkened, and the poet rapidly moves toward one of the most memorable images in *Paterson*—radium.

Early in Book 1, Williams lays down the working principle of *Paterson* as well as a key process in atomic physics itself. "Divorce is / the sign of knowledge in our time / Divorce! Divorce! / with the roar of the river / forever in our ears." It is oversimplification perhaps to see atomic development as mere parting, in a more and more profound fashion, of seemingly inseparable matter. Yet so many of the early breakthroughs—from Rutherford's first bombardment of nitrogen with alpha particles through Chadwick's discovery of that all-purpose bullet, the neutron—activate, metaphorically, the poet's new formula, his template for understanding. That Williams was thrilled with the methodology of the atomic process shows itself not only from what we know of his early reading but also in his admiration of such men as Vannevar Bush, Roosevelt's advisor and the head of the atomic bomb project, whom he met in 1946. "That man Bush," he wrote to his friend Joseph Steeler, "was the most interesting to me. It is amazing what he and his associates have accomplished—looked at simply as brains." Whatever Williams's feeling at this time concerning the dangerous aspects of atomic research, his delight in its theoretical nerve is clear. In *Paterson*, the poet's wish to shake the current order, cutting barebone to "the radiant gist," flashes with an optimism neither political nor economic but largely spiritual.

The need to break, to divide, to isolate in the search for essence: no idea in *Paterson* is staged with more dramatic sense. Although Williams returns to the source of the miraculous—the actual discovery of radium by Marie Curie in 1898—invoking its real history in Book 4, this fact lies at the end of an evocation begun in Book 3, in which the poet works to bring us visually and metaphorically to the purity of the scientific idea and finally to its intensity.

> . . . is there no release?
> Give it up. Quit it. Stop writing
> "Saintlike" you will never
>
> separate that stain of sense an offense
> to love, the mind's worm eating
> out the core, unappeased
>
> —never separate that stain
> of sense from the inert mass, never
>
> never that radiance
>   quartered apart
> unapproachable by symbols.

The poet's desire for release, pressing as it does against an assumption of religious imagery, brings this section almost to the point of prayer. In that darkened air, the "radiant gist" dazzles us all the more with its unapproachable distance. This, of course, is movement absolutely romantic, charged with the despair of the unattainable. And

Williams, timing his descent in this way, prepares us brilliantly for the sudden ascent into fact, Curie's real-life discovery coming in Book 4, so bringing the question to startling fruition, and closer to the point which will make that separation, that fission possible.

With homey detail, Williams enlivens the physical world of the find. "[A] fifth floor room, bread / milk and chocolate, a few / apples and coal to be carried / *des briquettes*, their special smell, / at dawn: Paris." The day is common, as pitchblende is not, yet the urge toward the impossible work at hand touches us by the irrepressible growth of its shape, layer to deeper layer: " —a furnace, a cavity aching / toward fission, a hollow / a woman waiting to be filled." The discontent of the earlier section takes particular form at last. In real enclosure—the room, the furnace, the woman, the mind—"dissonance" reveals itself to the dark: "after months, a failure, a / nothing. And then, returning in the / night, to find it. / LUMINOUS!"

This moment's beauty—Curie's approach, the dim, near-dawn room, the slow revelation of the radiant metal so famous that school-children remember its lit presence long after the lesson fades—depends upon its terror. The vast implication of that gleaming moment perhaps was sensed that evening—surely in Williams's hindsight it was—yet what that steady glow in the Parisian darkness would mean, what new intelligence it would press, was utterly unknown either then or, largely, now. Adds Williams with care, with a certain fear: "knowledge, the con-tainment / uranium, the complex atom, breaking down, / a city in itself."

Williams's awe before the fact of the atom, its dramatic fission, the creative dissolution toward which his earlier confusion ached, is lib-erated through the force of Curie's discovery. Yet in the momentary calm, a new uncertainty takes hold. Is it Williams the physician, seek-ing at this point of separation a way of synthesis, who realizes the imbalance? "And love," he writes, "bitterly contesting / waits / that the mind shall declare itself not / alone in dreams." So the poet deepens into the later work, "Asphodel, that Greeny Flower."

~

The flower itself, the asphodel, is ancient. Surely Williams knew this. From the Greek meaning "king's spear" or "scepter," it was sacred to Persephone, among others, and was often linked with the afterlife where the shades wandered and never found solace. The woman I reached by telephone at the Chicago Botanical Society told me simply, with nothing untoward in her voice: "In Greece, it's wild. And always connected with waste places and the dead." In fact, I recall hearing once that in the ancient world, asphodel was commonly planted near tombs; the dead preferred it since the roots were edible. The living chose to bake them first, according to Hippocrates and Pliny. In short, the flower was fully haunted long before Williams found it. Its development through the long poem that takes its name taps into that depth, into its seemingly endless dark.

For it is in "Asphodel" that Williams reaches directly and most ominously into the effect of nuclear fission, not only upon the human imagination but on man's whole capacity to perceive. Still, the poem itself, begun suddenly on a New York hotel restaurant menu in 1952 as a part of the final book of *Paterson* but actually written as a separate piece over the first half of that decade, remains first and last a work about love and, in that tradition, one of the greatest, said Auden, in the English language. Such an origin creates its unique "field," the generous space in which the voice operates, admitting readily even the underside of experience. "We lived long together / a life filled, / if you will, / with flowers. So that / I was cheered / when I came first to know / that there were flowers also / in hell." Such knowledge is gregarious and strange, insisting on an associative technique that flashes everywhere. Thus are the moves in the poem, rapid-fire, almost miming the swift chain reaction of hydrogen upon hydrogen atom.

In this restless pattern, Williams passes easily from declaration to recollection, from simple narrative—"when I was a boy / I kept a book /

to which . . . / I added pressed flowers"—to sudden interpretation—
"the asphodel / forebodingly / among them"—shifts triggered by the
real qualities of the governing image: the odor of flowers, their color, but
perhaps most memorably, in the case of the asphodel, its shape, its tall
spiked flowerhead revered since prehistory. The constant passage of
similar forms—from flower to phallus to atomic cloud—leads to profound connectives. "What do I remember / that was shaped / as this
thing is shaped?" Williams asks in what is, for me at least, his most
memorable and resonant question.

Yet in all the motion, a great isolation enters the poem from the
first, fueling the search and narrowing the issue. "There is something / something urgent / I have to say to you." As the poet rises to
that point of news, an analytic rhythm enters. "So to know, what I
have to know / about my own death, / if it be real, / I have to take it
apart." Echoing this process, previous divisions return. The split
between heart and head, an imbalance suggested in *Paterson* by
Curie's discovery, reaches now to a larger, more specific analogy, the
end result of Curie's troubling knowledge, the fact of the bomb.

The image first is one of irrepressible intelligence far outdistanc-
ing our means to understand, and Williams approaches it, not unnat-
urally, as a writer. What strikes him initially is its effect upon poetry's
traditional domain, that sense of unapproachable and mysterious
interior. "The poem / if it reflects the sea / reflects only / its dance /
upon that profound depth / where / it seems to triumph. / The bomb
puts an end / to all that." It is a remarkable insight from a strictly technical view. Here is matter in its barely discernible core abruptly, violently severed. Against that is the poem's habit of synthesis, things *like*
each other, a similar shape and motion of understanding, beyond the
simple squeeze of metaphor. In Williams's strange swift vision, such
insight is stilled, the poem's dance of "triumph" more than irrelevant.
By its killing thrust through the interior of things, the bomb corners
the heart and all passage toward it. How far we are this moment from

that July day in 1948 when Williams looked to this weapon for light and crucial direction. Yet the bomb's influence in "Asphodel" grows wider and more insidious.

Part of that influence is its beauty, if awe and fear can so translate; the bomb, as fact and image, takes us not exactly to the point of denial but to the point of numbness, a stillness that both empties and fills. Like Williams nearing one of his flowers, one almost forgets its sinister intent. "I should have known / though I did not, / that the lily-of-the-valley / is a flower makes many ill / who whiff it." It was like this at Los Alamos too, I remember reading; those present for that first atomic test later recalled, one after another, the same massive heat and light and sound. In Robert Oppenheimer's now legendary account, it was a passage of the *Bhagavad-Gita* that leapt to mind: "If the radiance of a thousand suns / were to burst into the sky / that would be like / the splendor of the Mighty One." And directly, as he watched the ominous cloud take form, a line of Sri Krishna came back: "I am Death, the shatterer of worlds." Such power—kin to deity, inspiring in us—what? Wrote Williams with simple silencing poise,

> I am reminded
> > that the bomb
> > > also
> is a flower
> > dedicated
> > > howbeit
> to our destruction.
> > The mere picture
> > > of the exploding bomb
> fascinates us
> > so that we cannot wait
> > > to prostrate ourselves
> before it.

To this he adds a startling corollary: "We do not believe / that love / can so wreck our lives."

And this leap, this transference? I keep turning it over. The love of knowledge, possibly, which produced the technical design that so touched Williams in its simplicity and potency, or the love traditionally imagined behind the terrifying power of a Judeo-Christian or Islamic god? One could draw light too from another poem in the same collection, "The Drunk and the Sailor," where the speaker, witnessing a fistfight, remarks finally: "I saw red / wanted to strangle the guy. / The fury of love / is no less." I'd go with this intensity as the starting point, the "shape" of Williams's connecting current. For if the bomb "puts an end" to poetry by alone divining final mystery, it also dashes the familiar steps to that understanding—a sense of human time, past and future crowding into our experience of the present, adding depth and hope. In the self-sufficient "fury" of its moment, the bomb, like love, stuns us into a singular belief—*this is it, nothing else*—an equally pure realization, yet one that releases not love's continuing spirit but death's final private throe. "They believe rather / in the bomb," Williams concludes, "and shall die by / the bomb."

This immediate shift of past and future must by definition jolt poetry even further but not—apparently—as Williams had wished. For him, the alteration of structure was a necessary step ensuring the future of poetry. At the University of Washington he had countered, partly for this reason, Eliot's decision to work within the traditions of the culture. "We are in a different phase—a new language—we are making the mass in which some later Eliot will dig. We must *see* our opportunity and increase the hoard others will find to use." But his sense of mission so real in 1948, when many physicists also held on to a thread of what could be called pre-H-bomb optimism, seems to have eroded to the point of helplessness in "Asphodel." Inevitably, the shadow deepens over the "measure" upon which Williams based not only the poem but the whole of our capacity to grasp who we are and how we live. The discoveries of new time and new space would set minds free, Williams thought, "dancing / to a new measure, / a new measure!" which subsequent news diminished. "Soon lost. / The measure itself / has been lost / and we suffer for it / we come to our deaths / in silence. / The bomb speaks."

In "Asphodel," Book 3, this profound uncertainty underscores and initiates a range of current from the strange and authentic stop-start invocation to Flossie, in which Williams demands the forgive-ness of love, to the vivid disclosure of the man in the subway who so reminds the poet of his own father. "But at once / the car grinds to a halt. / Speak to him, / I cried. He / will know the secret." Of course, it's no use; one can't fall back on the past for reassurance. It's a foreign place, but such distance blocks the future as well. "He was gone / and I did nothing about it. / With him / went all men / and all women too / were in his loins." This awareness of loss doubles the resulting isola-tion in that speeding subway car, in the relentless motion of the twen-tieth century, in the plain roaring of life itself. How brilliant then is Williams's shift to the personal, associating back to where this section began, not demanding but asking now for forgiveness, for reunion with the one loved.

In this vulnerable state, Williams takes the poem into its coda, its most visionary movement and the one toward which years of hope and confusion—plainly seeded in part by the atomic presence—have edged. Say simply: this is great poetry, the poet suddenly, urgently gaining strength and beginning again to weave with Jesuitical verve and human love a simple cure for our suicidal age. *Make it new*, drummed Pound. Williams listens and half-listens. "Then follows / what we have dreaded," he begins, "but it can never / overcome what has gone before." There is no stopping, it seems, the doom curiosity has seeded yet curiosity, that hopeful thing, that *desire*, could— must—govern what "follows." It is a moment of stasis that Williams clears out for us with such logic. "Do not hasten / laugh and play / in an eternity / the heat will not overtake the light. / That's sure," he says. "That gelds the bomb / permitting that the mind contain it."

The power of the mind to control matter builds upon an equation previously mentioned by Williams and surely returns to his early faith in the workings of science. "Are facts not flowers," he wildly argues, "and flowers facts / or poems flowers / or all works of the imagination, / interchangeable?" That we can ultimately invent or reinvent the world is the base rock on which the future depends. The shouted line comes quickly now in the fury of rescue—"Only the imagination is real!"—an idea Williams evidences by a more concrete realization. "If a man die / it is because death / has first / possessed his imagination."

It is from that death, from that vision of loss—this personal and universal Armageddon—that Williams speaks. An alliance rapidly forms, imagination associated directly with love that "will blossom," Williams predicts, in "that sweetest interval" of the immediate as the mind distances or "gelds" the bleaker possibilities. Both are, after all, "of a piece / swift as the light / to avoid destruction."

This peculiar light, mixed now for the first time with the "gelded" light of the atom, suffuses the poem, and courage grows in the poet, who borrows the sense outright from an ancient imagery whose high language and cadence we know in our bones. "So let us love / confident as is the light / in its struggle with darkness." Moving back, the poet discovers one of the richest images of intuitive sight: "The palm goes / always to the light." In this sign, there is release, the poem nearing its final line of proof. It's all assurance now: "Call it what you may! / The light / for all time shall outspeed / the thunder crack."

In the shadow of that hand, the poet rouses to the original personal focus of this quest—the immediacy of that first felt moment, not of dissolution or separation but of his wedding day. Williams's final orchestration is one of union, triggered simply by a flight back to the beginning stance of marriage and the innocence that produced it.

> Asphodel
>> has no odor
>>> save to the imagination
> but it too
>> celebrates the light.
>>> It is late
> but an odor
>> as from our wedding
>>> has revived for me
> and begun again to penetrate
>> into all crevices
>>> of my world.

It is, as Paul Mariani has pointed out, a leap obliterating time with "the rapidity of nuclear fission . . . bending back on itself like Einsteinian light." Further, the gathering force of the whole poem, now the voice breathlessly alert, poised into the coda, nearly dissolves the movement, matter breaking down to gas, to thin air, specific memory into pure reaction, sensation, satisfaction, this asphodel crushed to produce finally one lingering, powerful scent. The "odor" from flower, from imagination, from love, becomes the force that "has revived" the poet, again to "penetrate" his vision and thus neutralize potential destruction.

This power of the mind to transcend history—this "light" that Williams promises will "overtake" the "heat" of a thing that, once split, could propel us to a terrible end—is the resolution we long to hear. *Is it true? Can we trust him?* Regardless, Williams's reason carries us as he reaches back not to the thing itself under whose enormous shadow we shrink but back behind that, to the thing which produced it—the spirit of physics, which is the spirit of the imagination, of poetry, of love, the mind's "odor" of vitality. Williams's conviction seems to astonish even him. And that is the joy that breaks in the ending lines.

~

Those ending lines, written under the bomb's continuing threat, written by the poet in his seventies, recent survivor of a heart attack, three strokes, in and out of blindness, typing with one hand, make this piece—this *asphodel*, this-food-for-the-dead as the Greeks once saw it—a small miracle, a triumph in both personal and public ways. If we look back through it, see it as *lens*, telescopic and transporting, it suddenly becomes difficult to dismiss outright the Williams of 1948, who, full-hearted in his vision of breakneck change in poetry, held up the bomb as example, as astrolabe and compass, long past what we can politely or morally bear, past Nagasaki and Hiroshima. For in the method behind its discovery, that inquiry into the new, the dangerous, the poet saw the human mind in what he considered its finest motion. "This isn't optimism"—I picture him again in Seattle, his words as certain as mantra—"it is chemistry; or better, physics." In fact, Williams was wrong that afternoon. Optimism it remains, an eye wide to a future full of—possibly—happy circumstance; he extracts even this essence out of the moral agony in "Asphodel," going finally for the spirit of science, past and—one realizes—in spite of the momentary and destructive letter of its law.

What becomes easy to dismiss is Williams's protestation of indifference to "the great world," which, as he said, "never interested me much." In *Paterson* and more fully in "Asphodel," Williams leaps into the central historic quandary of his century; more, he was perhaps the modern poet most conscious of and dependent upon his time, its "radiant gist"—in music, in painting, and, of course, in science—to guide his work. His assumption that the writer be inevitably *in* the world and responsible *for* it is an idea from which Williams never strays. "On the poet devolves the most vital function of society," he wrote years earlier, "to recreate it—the collective world—in times of stress, in a new mode, fresh in every part, and so set the world working, or dancing, or murdering each other again, as may be."

It is, not surprisingly, an odd assurance.

POETS IN CARS

Begin at the end, near Lebanon, Indiana, forty minutes south of West
Lafayette on I-65. It's a big enough road, crossing this place where the
glacier ground down whatever wild formation reigned twelve thousand years ago to this flat green kingdom, bean fields or snowy stub-
ble depending on where we are, which month, which moment on our
eternal orbit around the sun. And here's what I see on the horizon,
this distant sign: *Wrecks—Drive Carefully. We Meet by Accident.*
Below, the barbed-wire fence goes on for a mile or two. Behind that,
yes, the biggest automobile graveyard in Indiana, maybe the Midwest.
From here, on 65, the wrecking yard seems small, really nothing to
speak of. But—*you have no idea*, to coin a phrase.

The idea I had concerned getting a simple headlight, cheap, for
our '87 Dodge Colt. I called up that morning. The guy checked his
computer (his computer!). *Sure, sure, no problem.* It was fall. The
fields—not green, not snowy, just plain sepia, exhausted amid the
final ravishment of color, those reds and blazing yellows from the few
stands of trees about. I took the big road to the narrow road that eventually turned to pure gravel and stopped. I was given a map in the
filthy office, this thing in my hand like an old drawing of a nineteenth-
century town, some hopeful, smart guy's idea of the place, the town—
what's the word?—*platted*, everything tidy and formal, a sweet,
shrunken abstraction of the great *polis*. Except instead of houses on
corners and built row by row, in my mad blueprint cars were blocked

in, hand-lettered—a 1975 Chrysler here, a 1985 Toyota wagon there, a Rambler from 1991 two cars down and one truck over.

Why I got the map at all, I'm not sure, since I clearly needed a guide to this underworld, a kid in a ripped T-shirt, it turned out, who waved me back to the gravel where we climbed into a barely working blue Honda, minus doors, backseat, the trunk smashed dizzily into nothing-like-a-trunk. But it did drive or at least the kid managed it though the car spit and raged as we lurched forward down streets actually named Maple and Sunrise and Elm, the pastoral dream of a town wasted, blocks upon blocks, past crazy into tragic, its "houses," of course, these cars bashed in or nearly folded in half, just sitting there, windshields gone, doors off hinges, seats missing. Then we turned a corner and there, the evil twin of my Dodge Colt, right down to its color, gray, a twisted fun-house mirror image of my car, the horrible *after* picture of my "in happier times" version parked quietly at home. Was it weird? Yes. And the kid leapt out with a screwdriver and expertly, matter-of-factly, dug out its headlight. *The left one, right?* he said. I nodded, numb to it all. Was this the past? Or the future? Or neither? Had we just passed over the dark waters of Lethe? Was I asleep? Was I awake? "What's it like, doing this every day?" I asked the kid as we drove back to the office. "Well, a lot of guys get religion, working here," he said. And then: "Me, I don't know."

I don't know either. It's a chill, though, each time I pass that place now on my occasional trips to Indianapolis. I forget and then remember all those cars—those not-quite-cars-anymore—lined up in dreamlike parody of what passes for civilization: the New England village, the sleepy midwestern town. There's the obvious, melodramatic movie to play back for each—the car *before* impact, kids quarreling in the back, then the sudden, high contrast cut to the twisted afterlife of bent metal and broken glass, its value now only in stray still-working particulars dug out by a guy with a screwdriver or by someone like me, collecting images that overwhelm and humble and sicken. Graverobbers, all of us.

And the car as image? As metaphor or state of mind? Hero or monstrosity of pure poetic motion? I recall a guy I heard about in my twenties, supposedly brilliant, full of promise, survivor for a time of almost daily hits of LSD who finally went mad because he couldn't grasp what a car was, would stare at one for hours until his amazement turned to terror. I'm not sure I believe this story. But certain tensions do shine darkly to rattle us, the car's calm against possible violence, euphoria, or grief, its promise of both routine and adventure.

Even pulled back from its death-mask extremes, there's a powerful workaday wonder in our notion of the car that enlarges even as it strips us down. Coming late to all this—I didn't learn to drive until I was thirty-seven—I remember a small shock as I spun out into traffic the first time: *I had never been alone in a moving car.* A certain innocence dropped away. Who was I now? In a very early poem, Robert Bly memorably defines the car as "this solitude covered with iron." It's a peculiarly ironic and American way of meditation, our solitary *sitting*, our *za-zen*, this moving through space at incredible speeds, a brute, dangerous force, so many cars flooding the road. Which is to say, though there may be hundreds of us jammed together on highways or city streets, making this a community of sorts—Tomas Tranströmer has called this "a torpid, glittering dragon. / I am a scale on that dragon"—each, nevertheless, can be perfectly alone, monkish and oblivious in "the small world of the car" as Bly puts it earlier in his poem. When I think like this, the whole 2,000-pound business engineered around me gets stranger, light as lace and as fragile. And I'm driving—where was it I had to go?—nothing in my head now, nothing at all.

∽

Which may be where poetry begins, in that deep, expansive privacy where we believe—trust—something will happen in that forward motion. Maybe it's just pure kinetics that gives confidence, the body moving however it can through time and space. No doubt there's a history to this in poetry, back to prehistory, definitely pre-car, pre-bus, pre-anything-with-a-motor. Consider the romantic poets so smitten with the *walk* as occasion for their work, those solitary and communal rambles through the British Lake District and beyond, Wordsworth most famously writing all of his "Tintern Abbey," more properly, his "Lines Composed a Few Miles above Tintern Abbey on Revisiting the Banks of the Wye during a Tour, July 13, 1798," writing literally *as he walked*, claiming nothing added that night or in the days that followed. Some seventy years later, it's Hopkins too, wandering about on holiday in Switzerland, first in the towns ("But Basel at night! with a full moon waking the river and sending up straight beams from the heavy clouds that overhung it . . .") and then in the Alpine countryside ("How fond of and warped to the mountains it would be easy to become! For every cliff and limb and edge has its own nobility. Two boys came down the mountain yodeling . . ."). In our own time, A. A. Ammons wrote straight out that the poem *is* a walk, pointing out how both use body and mind, both turn and *return* fully individual in shape, intent, duration, the self magnified and quirky, in charge. But there's something about moving *and* watching that shifts this last distinction a bit. In fact, the self shrinks down in our great press to keep going; it's the world that looms up around us made of odd, sticking details. All of which opens the lyric impulse, now something not simply all-about-me but cut with an epic expansion, glimpses profoundly *other* rushing in—human, nonhuman, both. We can't absorb it fast enough.

Surely Whitman comes into this with a bang, volume up, that exclamatory everywhere-I-look-I-see forward pitch to so much of his work. His walkabouts often begin as just that and deeply structure the actual shape of his thinking, cast first as an easy stroll through one teeming city scene after another, the sights apparently real—that is, right there on the street—then the other kind, remembered or imagined, the stuff of back rooms and eavesdrop and dream. So it becomes poetry, that uneasy balance between what is interior and *out there*, two worlds and so much of each. It's partly the sheer bulk of Whitman's work that astonishes. In "Song of Myself," we get tireless observation in brief hit after hit; "It is only a list—but what a list!" Randall Jarrell once exclaimed. There's the girl at her sewing machine, then a shoe-maker waxing his thread or the peddler sweating under his pack or the conductor beating time. Then come paving men, roofers, fare collectors, prostitutes bedraggled in their shawls, opium-eaters with their "just opened lips," each given their own long, lumbering spot-light of a line to be tableaued for a moment before the poet/speaker turns the corner.

With such accumulation we get weight, we get strangeness, more so because Whitman before long seems bored with simply walking down the street and peering through walls. Soon, interspersed among these gritty city images, the whole continent is fair game. All at once it's unnervingly like those Discovery Channel productions about ancient civilizations that show vast complicated designs cut into the earth, which make sense only when seen from high in the air, an impossible feat for the time. *Who really did this?* a sonorous voice intones. Just so, Whitman is dizzily everywhere. We see a trapper in Michigan, for instance, deckhands docking steamboats, raccoon hunters in Tennessee and Arkansas, the president himself holding a cabinet meeting while—at the same moment?—a squatter in his western forest "strikes deep with an axe." I'm only talking one poem from *Leaves of Grass* here, one section out of—count them—fifty-two, before Whitman, in his closing lines, actually takes a breath. But that's not true either. "I depart as air," he tells us, ending the poem with only a promise of stillness. "Failing to fetch me at first keep encouraged, / Missing me one place search another, / I stop some-where waiting for you."

Whitman went beyond the simple walk, though, absorbing all the new inventions, trains particularly, their speed and noise. And he's famous for a trip made by steamboat to New Orleans, an experience that Paul Zweig claims changed him into a poet. Guy Davenport has tantalized us with the thought that Whitman's lurching, long-lined rhythms mirror those of the nineteenth century's rough buckboards and carriages that reduced distance and inspired the dreamer to whatever *elsewhere* ahead, a habit no doubt linked to the optimism and transcendental leanings of the time. Meaning: Whitman had his eye and ear to it, *this* world in all its moving parts. That he started with the *walk* to pace and even shape his poems makes sense in the most natural and even democratic way. But a new force, some mechanized *other* was coming into the mix, turning it faster, more chaotic, something that had less and less to do with being human.

When Elizabeth Bishop wrote to her favorite aunt, Grace Bowers, in 1972, it was partly to report that she had finished it finally, the poem dedicated to that aunt and long in the works, almost twenty years. "That damned poem," she complained. Because getting it *"written"*— she underlined that one—in time to read at the Harvard commencement had kept her from visiting her aunt at home in Nova Scotia, a place Bishop loved and where she had spent much of her childhood. "It is called 'The Moose,'" she wrote, assuring her, in light of the poem's dedication—and one can imagine the poet's pleasure in this— "you are *not*" (underlined again) "the moose."

And what *was* the moose? Simply itself, an honest-to-god moose, stepping out on the road after dark to stop a bus cold and accept the travelers' awe and admiration, a true story that Bishop transformed with a feel for real time and hallucinatory event. In the process, the poem gradually gives homage to the unknown, to surprise, to strangeness. The experience itself, had he been on that bus, was something Whitman might have cast in the laudatory, reverent way he reserved for so many things; not exactly "To a Locomotive in Winter" perhaps, with its archaic rise and repetitions—"Thy metrical, now swelling pant and roar, now tapering in the distance. / Thy great protruding head-light fixed in front"—but close. Bishop's words though—"Towering, antlerless / high as a church"—wouldn't be too off the mark for him, a start anyway.

What matters a great deal, I think, is that this ghostly creature ("a moose has come out of / the impenetrable wood / and stands there / looms rather") is seen from a moving bus that has suddenly stopped and not, say, from some lawn chair across the road or through a safe kitchen window a short distance away. There's dynamic history behind the moment; we're *in* it and we've been there for a while— which intensifies everything. Here, after all, it's not just any bus but one passing through complex and intricate worlds. It's moved from dusk to dark, afternoon fog to moonlight, village after farm after village where vivid details rise up abrupt and surreal and fragmented: sweet peas "on wet white string," rubber boots "illuminated and solemn" left outside, a collie with one bark and "the smell of salt hay," images as ephemeral as the "pale flickering" of a woman shaking out her tablecloth after supper, and as evocative. Bishop's generous unmelodramatic take is immediate and present tense, credible; a shifting, complicated vision fully in keeping with her first ambition for poetry, worked out very early when, still a student at Vassar, she wanted to make poems "in action" and not "at rest," the latter sort, she wrote to a friend, "occupying properly almost the entire history and field of poetry," adding later that, "if I have any talent, it is along these narrow lines."

Her exceptions to that "almost . . . entire history and field of poetry" were George Herbert and most particularly Gerard Manley Hopkins, whose eccentric work largely wasn't of the ponderous "at rest" variety where every notion was thought through a thousand times before it was written down. Instead Hopkins opted to "time" his work differently, Bishop wrote in a college essay, "to stop his poems, set them on paper, at the point in their development where they are still incomplete, still close to the first kernel of truth or apprehension that gave rise to them." I have to say I like that a lot, like that it's perfectly okay to stop the syllogism at any point, that it's not crucial to push reasonably through to a final orchestration, to the "therefore, Socrates is a fish" part; there are other ways of triumph. Such an approach is *almost* reflective, but not quite; its weight is first dramatic—enacted *right now* and sequential—coming out of someplace, en route to someplace else, the feel of a lived life. Until, of course, everything stops.

How do you get there? a friend of mine in college loved to say. First, you go there! he'd answer himself jubilantly, every time. In Ammons's discussion of the walk, as much as motion is heralded, he eventually admits it's finally about getting back to a "non-verbal source" in poems, "motion to no-motion, to the still point of contemplation and deep realization." So the power of that wrecking yard near Indianapolis drifts back, the way calm and a certain timelessness was returned to those cars, frozen at the twisted second of collision.

It's not always a matter of grief, such wrenching out of routine. In Bishop's poem, by the jolt of the driver stopping his bus and killing his lights, it's suddenly a visitation, the mere mortals on board snatched out of sleepy, forward-roaring, ordinary time into sacred time, one they can't quite grasp. The moose "looms," after all. And "why, why do we feel / (we all feel) this sweet / sensation of joy?" Bishop asks as— "curious creature," the driver whispers—it approaches and "sniffs at / the bus's hot hood." It's a standoff, a coiled moment. The best thing? Bishop simply *lets it be*. Ammons, in the same essay, gives us reason for such method: "The greatest wrong that can be done a poem is to substitute a known part for an unknown whole." To make it reasonable, I guess he means, tidy and locked in so we *get* it. Here, in Bishop's poem, the great *otherness* of the moose is undisturbed. One is allowed to witness the mystery, just that. She allows it, in short, to unfold. As a result, we keep staring down that road as *who we are*, unfinished and—dare we even think it?—mysterious ourselves. The bus starts moving again. Has the poem ended? That seems an illusion.

One can consider William Stafford's "Traveling through the Dark" in a similar fashion or Jane Kenyon's "The Sick Wife," though for both poems the way is far bleaker. Stafford's piece, probably his greatest hit, seems year by year more pointed as our cities grow greedily past their boundaries, farms and forests shrinking and more animals killed by speeding, oblivious traffic. Its small scene—the speaker stopping his car at night to investigate a deer dead in the road, "stiffened already" but huge, her fawn inside "alive, still, never to be born"—belies how large the poem is, cutting to the heart of what it means to live in America, to drive a car here, to see almost daily the clash of human-made and natural worlds, complexities that we neither control nor fully grasp and, most days, ignore regardless of our uneasiness with it all. But circumstance has forced the issue here. Stafford subtly owns up to everything but with none of the moral cant and implied self-congratulation that lesser writers might bring to it. "Beside that mountain road I hesitated," he writes, still mulling it over himself, thus making us think through the sad, impossible situation. But one cannot think, at least not yet.

> The car aimed ahead its lowered parking lights;
> under the hood purred the steady engine.
> I stood in the glare of the warm exhaust turning red;
> around our group I could hear the wilderness listen.

Something Randall Jarrell admired about Whitman was his way of keeping "contradictory elements" in his work. He worried that if poets "organize" such things out, gone are exactly what makes poems "represent us—as logical and methodical generalizations cannot—our world and our selves, which are also full of contradictions." The "steady engine" here purring away against the "wilderness" and, by inference, the dying deer; the "lowered parking lights" against the dark: these images set tragedy down where it actually lives, in the warring priorities of our common life. "I thought hard for us all,—my only swerving—" Stafford says, probably the most memorable line he wrote, "then pushed her over the edge into the river."

Jane Kenyon's "The Sick Wife," the last poem she wrote before her death from leukemia in 1995, is another small marvel of giant proportions. Like Stafford, she allows the contradictions to stand and, like Bishop (and Hopkins behind her), keeps her images close to "the first kernel of truth or apprehension that gave rise to them." Here again is a car but this time stopped in a parking lot, the "sick wife" waiting there, already a kind of ghostly presence while her husband shops for groceries. "Not yet fifty, / she has learned what it's like / not to be able to button a button," Kenyon tells us but doesn't linger on such infirmities. There's too much world outside of the car to read. We see now with great intimacy through the sick wife's eyes although the whole piece is curiously distant, cast in third person. Yet small things are caught with such longing that a kind of catalog takes over, images of well-being thrown up in contrast to what must be, we imagine, the stricken view of the sick wife who watches. A straightforward, exhausted sweetness infuses it all.

> It was the middle of the day—
> and so only mothers with small children
> or retired couples
> stepped through the muddy parking lot.
>
> Dry cleaning swung and gleamed on hangers
> in the cars of the prosperous.
> How easily they moved—
> with such freedom,
> even the old and relatively infirm.

Kenyon's empathic acknowledgment of the line between illness and health, put down in the poem plainly and without melodrama, suggests Chekhov's matter-of-fact richness. And what everyday object—the dry cleaning here—ever *meant* more eloquently? But it's the final stanza that manages the amazing. First, disappearance is registered in the most natural, unnerving way possible—"The windows begin to steam up." Against that, a wild breaking away, something only a car can do with enough authority and indifference to cut all human bonds.

> The cars on either side of her
> pulled away so briskly
> that it made her sick at heart.

The overall shape is the exact reverse of Bishop's and Stafford's poems and, for that matter, of Ammons's plan for poems too; it's no-motion, then motion, that leave a life behind. And which carries more terror and beauty in Kenyon's poem—the delicacy or the ruthlessness? And how even to talk about such a merging?

The *stopped* vehicle in these poems—Bishop's bus, Stafford's and Kenyon's cars—and the deep melancholy in those images, especially in the latter two, is close to iconic in our poetry. Two forces—one forward moving, unthinking, one stilled and reflective—connect and disconnect us; the uneasy match seems profoundly American. Even Theodore Roethke, whose images align themselves more commonly with the natural world—his roses and fieldmice, his elm's "twittering, restless cloud" filled with orioles—wrote of such yes/no movement, a stalled car then its stopping altogether to launch "The Far Field" section of his "North American Sequence," one of his most troubling visions, lines, I've found, that a lot of people—sometimes surprising themselves—know by heart. What *is* it about this passage? Cast in a kind of dream time, the scene is of "driving alone, without luggage, out on a long peninsula." And Roethke keeps at it.

The road lined with snow-laden second growth,
A fine dry snow ticking the windshield,
Alternate snow and sleet, no on-coming traffic,
And no lights behind, in the blurred side-mirror,
The road changing from glazed tarface to a rubble of stone,
Ending at last in a hopeless sand-rut,
Where the car stalls,
Churning in a snowdrift
Until the headlights darken.

It's difficult to shake such images; their hard natural detail over-whelms and defeats. But it's the way this poem begins that startles us in quite another way. "I dream of journeys repeatedly," Roethke writes. And who doesn't feel the thrill of such a line? One thinks down and back. And something enormous opens.

～

How big is it really, this unsettling mix of plenitude and vulnerability, this near hypnotic wish to push onward? How much of it *is* dream? The idea of journey takes us back to Whitman—can we ever really shake this guy?—his vast reach, his sense of the American expanse, a huge country, after all, equal to the epic nature of *journey*, the word itself. He set a lens for others to look through, a window easily caulked into the car once it was invented.

It's a predictable step to put Allen Ginsberg first after Whitman in this great moving chain of being. "If I had a Green Automobile," he wrote to Neal Cassady in an early poem, "we'd batter up the cloudy highway / where angels of anxiety / careen through trees / and scream out of the engines." This green automobile, he says later, is given "in flight / a present, a present / from my imagination." As much as *escape* is lovingly offered in such lines, a more recent and sober take is Lucia Perillo's. In her poem, "The Northside at Seven,"

such a "cloudy highway" recovers and grounds and, whatever the
sad price, goes for reason, not release.

> I forget so much. I forget why tears come on the freeway,
> mornings I drive by these old buildings when bread is
> cooking—
> why? for what? Sometimes I feel history slipping from my
> body
> like a guilty bone, & the only way to call it back
> is to slump behind the wheel. . . .

Another poet, Campbell McGrath, sometimes compared to Whitman in his energy and scope, might agree. He does, after all, seem
more often in his car than not in his poems, his numerous journeys
more a way of flight *back*—like Perillo's—to figure and reassess.
Behind the wheel in an early piece of McGrath's, for example, in
"Almond Blossoms, Rock and Roll, the Past Seen as Burning Fields,"
he gives us a half heroic, half mock-heroic flashback to a thoroughly
American road trip, this time managed in Europe with the young and
wily Hank, Dave, Ed, and, yes, the speaker, who "hunched in the shell
of the beaten, graffiti-winged bug / . . . scalped for 60 dollars in
Berlin" are "insanely happy, wild and lost, speed-mad" as they head
south. Does it matter that it's Europe? Or that history, called back as
Perillo would have it, still keeps slipping—as she feared it would—in
so many ways? "For us, all of Spain," McGrath tells us, "was like

> anywhere else, driving the Great Plains or Inland Empire,
> Los Banos, Buttonwillow, Bakersfield,
> familiar rhythm and cadence of the road,
> another car, another continent, another rope of lights
> slung along the San Joaquin Valley.
> I don't know if the rush we felt was culturally specific,

though it was the literal noise of our culture we rode
like Vandals or Moors toward a distant sea,
but that feeling was all we ever desired, that freedom
to hurtle madly against the sweet, forgiving flesh of the world,
urged on by stars and wind and music,
kindred spirits of the night.

As if coming out of dream, we're then cast upward into a quite different sense of things. "How the past / overwhelms us," McGrath writes, abruptly stopped and back from looking back, "violent as floodwaters, vivid as war."

This sense of grand overview, the euphoria and the sometime dark that accompanies it, has no doubt always been the imagination's province, carrying the epic's largely romantic impulse that can give breadth to the smallest lyric. Yet in poems that orbit the car, a new isolation comes into the mix as if, by some weird law of physics, what opens the world to endless discovery also closes it. In this thought we're back to Stafford's and even Kenyon's deep melancholy; even in McGrath's sweeping, fragmented vision, the light is sepia at best, memory's light, and through that, perhaps regret or something more weighted seeps in—Stafford works this large canvas too—a kind of cultural and historical rethinking. "What concerns me most . . . / is how glibly and with what myopia / we bore the mantle of individual liberty across the continents," McGrath tells us in retrospect, the reckless joy of the trip somehow *stopped* in the retelling, *used up*, a curious blankness—is it longing?—eventually staining everything. "You see," he concludes, "the brakes were gone and it wasn't our country . . . / And though we stood in the very shadow of the Rock of Gibraltar, / we never even noticed it. That's how I picture us still, / me and Ed and Dave on the ferry to Tangier, / laughing in our sunglasses, forgetting to look back."

For certain poets, the next step is closer to despair, the road trip completely minus the sweetness. I'm thinking of Weldon Kees, who, writing out of what Kenneth Rexroth called "a permanent and hopeless apocalypse" of his own, gave us some of the most austere and memorable poems in the twentieth century before his suicide or his secret expatriation to Mexico—in any case, his disappearance—in 1955. His "Travels in North America" maps a large-scale journey, actually many journeys, the poem a collage of various crossings and recrossings from Kansas City to Dalton, Georgia, to Santa Barbara to Evansville to Albuquerque to Boston and beyond. As in McGrath's poem, it's *remembered* time and, as such, carries the grainy light of dusk around it, late afternoon's peculiar stillness in spite of its perpetual motion. The voice here, as Donald Justice has said, is something "we have never heard before." It's beyond wistful into bitter, past unflappable into indifferent. In this, Justice insists, Kees is "original in one of the few ways that matter." And certainly what matters is how something this close to Whitman's rich catalog is not so much savored, image by image, as discarded. For Whitman, travel promised release and ecstatic self-discovery, his "Come forth!" in "Song of the Open Road," his "Out of the dark confinement! Out from behind a screen!" For Kees, such adventure is all about disappointment, missed chances, offering more evidence of the horrors or, seemingly worse, the banality of the world.

From the start, it's a brilliant downer: towns whose names are "unpronounceable"; motels where "well-fed moths . . . greet us from the walls"; where gulls drop down "to shiver gravely in the steady rain"; where even famous restaurants serve meals giving off "a classic taste of tin," and stars—this time near Santa Fe—are "old, discolored / by a milky haze." It goes larger, Kees's scathing genius eye touching history—"ruined pueblos" near Los Alamos where "tall, young men" guard the atom bomb. Over all, there's a brownish film "sticking to the windshields," the sky "raining soot" and those "television aerials" by the thousands as one drives by, not to mention the endless repetitions of a droning culture in how many *Joe's Lunches* or *Larry's Shoe Repairs* one finds, how many First, Main, and Market Streets that "fuse together" town after town until "you have forgotten singularities," or further, "forgotten why you left or why you came to where you are / Or by what roads and passages, / Or what it was, if anything, you were hoping for." Not exactly McGrath's blurred, energized notion that "Spain was like anywhere else." It's a litany of exhaustion out of "this space between oceans," as Kees calls it.

In such a moment, one could go back to William Carlos Williams, the unshakable claim closing out his poem "To Elsie" that it "Is only in isolate flecks that / something / is given off / No one / to witness / and adjust, no one to drive the car." Of course, there's a witness here, however darkly burdened. Kees ends at the water, on a beach of detritus—"spongy two-by-fours . . . mattresses and stones . . . tinned stuff with the labels gone" and, incredibly, a "sodden, fading" map of Brooklyn Heights, which triggers the poem's leap back in time where only the eternal present tense can rouse us. Now it's a January snow ten years earlier, a subway there. Then it's back to California, then the Cape with finally something soothing, its "washboard roads," its "summer light and dust" that lifts everything briefly before the poem closes us out even as it includes us in its great giving up. "And here," Kees writes in the last few lines, "now textured like a blotter, like the going years / and difficult to see, is where you are, and where I am, / and where the oceans cover us."

There's an awful irony working here. If there's a *before* and an *after* in *Leaves of Grass*, its good-hearted dream of the road, how close we are in Kees's poem to the aching *before* that Whitman wanted to free us from, that "secret silent loathing and despair" sensed "inside of dresses and ornaments, inside those washed and trimmed faces" at home, that certain "death under the breast-bone, hell under the skullbones" (a line Randall Jarrell especially loved), all things his spirited "Allons! Allons!" would forever destroy—if only we'd believe and come along.

That "hell under the skullbones"? Kees *lived* there. So much for the common wisdom: travel didn't broaden him; it somehow emptied this poet. Glimpses from a moving car remain just that, not dazzling shards that imply a complex world and narrative one cannot stay to understand but something forever limited and often sordid though, occasionally, a lovely bit slips in. "Warm in our room, we watched the bathers' breaths," the poet tells us about Santa Barbara in winter, the motel pool heated and therefore inviting. It's just that unlike Whitman, whose generous inclusion, despite his self-absorbed bravado, of so many others—workers, children, the dying, the wounded—makes *him* generous, Kees's recall of screaming girls at parties or "bridges choked with cars" or "yellow weeds like entrails," all seen in flickering array, ends up reducing him. But because every image, however grisly, seems accurate and true, it also oddly deepens him and, in the process, chills us to the bone. *Finally we are seeing things as they are*, we might think, thinking *this* vision out of *this* particular car window a rare, hard moment of clarity, thinking *don't get swayed—ever again—by any upbeat romantic drivel.*

"The windshield's full of tears," Ginsberg wrote.

There's a walk my husband and I sometimes take on Sundays, down the Wabash River Trail, mainly deep woods that follow first the river and, past that, the creek that once—180 years ago?—was big enough to sustain a mill. It's one of the few extended bits of wilderness in our part of Indiana, if you can call it wilderness. You can't; it's all at least second growth, and at times you can hear I-65 in the distance. But it's a beautiful place, the path crowded at its edges with jewelweed and ferns, poison ivy claiming tree trunks, and birds, of course, even an occasional deer startled and frozen, staring at us not thirty yards away.

Our favorite spot is ghostly, a place off trail where someone long ago abandoned four or five old cars. We marvel at how they got there in the first place, the trees large now, thickly placed. But then? Were the cars driven here? Or towed by truck? Thirty years ago, I'm sure it was an eyesore, an inkling of what a trash heap the trail was becoming. That didn't happen. Just the cars turned up, nothing else. More, so unlike those in the wrecking yard forty miles south of here, these cars, rust and shattered glass aside, are largely intact however spooky, making a still life of sorts, the woods slowly overtaking them, old silt from the flooded creek literally packing them into the earth itself, lush weeds growing out of windows, through doors, stray maple trees coming up through the flooring. It's a thing, as the German sociologist Georg Simmel wrote eighty years ago on the nature of the *ruin*, which might characterize peace for us, "our sense that two world potencies—the striving upward and the sinking downward—are finally working serenely together." Further, because of what the car *is*, there's a deeper fascination to the scene, an active however phantomlike sense of the car once in motion, our inevitable isolation behind the wheel combined with the powerful wish simply to go, to see, to connect.

Here we get entangled in another idea of Simmel's, this one about "the adventure," that part of our experience which "drops out" of life's continuity. Remembered later, the adventure "takes on the quality of a dream," though nevertheless deeply "connected to the center" in us, "an aspect of the inside." In such a connection, maybe we've never left poetry, which Donald Hall has so wonderfully called "inside person talking to inside person." Maybe. Probably. What I cherish in this notion is how the car, this mass-produced, universal object turned image, voted most-likely-to-become-a-cliché in every poll I've ever hallucinated is, in fact, a candidate for such privacy, an occasion in poems for original discovery of all kinds, even taking Ginsberg's line back to its ghost source in Virgil some two thousand years ago, into the "tears of things." And the cliché part? That's surely part of its power, the fact that we know this image inside out, past thinking.

I've heard it said that there are only two stories in the world: *a man goes on journey* and *a stranger comes to town*—same story, of course, but seen from opposite angles. Surely the car can be a presence in either. But you could mix things up. A *stranger* could go on a journey too. Which is to say, who else ever drives? Behind the wheel, don't we all get stranger and stranger to ourselves as the world swallows us? Out of one life, into another. Meanwhile, I know I keep half-dreaming certain lines, over and over. One of them is Bishop's as she ends her poem "Arrival at Santos" with a heart-stopping shift. "We leave Santos at once," she tells us. Then, so quietly: "We are driving to the interior."

My Head

This is the street where my head lives, smoking cigarettes. I pass here and see it lying half asleep on a windowsill on my way to school where I study microbiology, which I finally give up because it all seems too small to have very much meaning in a world which I attempt to live in.

Then I begin my studies in advanced physics, which entails trying to understand atoms and subatomic particles. I give this up too when I finally realize that I have entered a world even smaller than microbiology.

I think then that I should become an astronomer and open myself to the largest view, but see only dots, which the professor says any one of which might have taken millions, or perhaps billions, of years to reach only recently evolved optic nerves; and that in fact any star whose light we accept might be long perished, leaving only a long wistful string of light. And I wonder what this has to do with me or the world I attempt to live in. So I give up astronomy.

I come here now, into this street, looking up at my head lying half asleep on a windowsill, smoking cigarettes, blinking, and otherwise totally relaxed in the way men become when they have lost all hope . . .

—Russell Edson

EDSON'S HEAD

For those who write them, certain lines of poetry—often strange, inexplicable images—once they steal into the mind, cannot be extracted by civilized means. Distraction, for instance, cannot faze them. Doing laundry or reading or withstanding a slew of gregarious nonstop friends for a few days: nothing dislodges such images, partly because they are not spawned by ordinary experience but emerge fully birthed from nowhere. All poets, I'd guess, gladly take such curiosities on arrival or at least keep them iced somewhere to be savored later, coaxed beyond themselves to cross the stuff of daily life, often as analogies, into poems. Russell Edson, however, in his graceful twisted way, stays with his beginning governing line to invent a world; the image is, in the most primal frightening sense, a root. I'd say courage makes him do this and probably reverence. Poems for him are never mere running commentary on the grind of living; his vision is more complete and solitary than that. The first line of an Edson poem startles us, quite away from ourselves, into trance.

This is the street where my head lives, smoking cigarettes.

One can only proceed, as Edson certainly must, with absolute belief. Here is simply (simply?) a disembodied head casually alive, smoking a cigarette. This is also, incidentally, a single street out of an infinity of streets where the head keeps its vigil. The straightforward, matter-of-fact statement assumes a credibility beyond us. This *is*, after all, whether we like it or not. We are called to witness, not to understand or question. With the swiftness and clarity of a visual artist, which he also is, Edson offers us the thing itself: a head, half asleep, smoking cigarettes. The grotesque ancestry here—heads spiked and held aloft on warring poles, heads severed and shrunken for magic, garroted heads offered, in treaties, as payment—is muted but not overcome by the narrator's careful shrug. Without editorial comment, the violent image settles gently, in sure solitude like eclipsed light moments ago blinding, now in exacting slow shadow. The single sentence Edson allows is only a peripheral glance against the head's eerie permanence. Like the speaker, we move, quickly probably, on our way someplace else.

Where? Where else: to school. This is revision following vision, starting with zero or at least the very small: microbiology is what the speaker claims to study, then what is even smaller, atomic and subatomic particles inventing within *what-we-see* a furious, invisible world. Who is this speaker anyway—a Hans Castorp, a Huck Finn, a Holden Caulfield—looking to a future self who looks back at him calmly, over cigarettes? And how neglectfully prosaic Edson becomes in a willful tangle of phrases, rambling and subordinate as the speaker enters knowledge and leaves it, enters again and steps away—so much to study and then forget!—as though human thought were a hot bath and the telephone rings us out of it for more important news.

I think then that I should become an astronomer and open myself to the largest view. . . .

"I think then," says the speaker, and we are passing through time as though days and decisions were bright transparencies to flip over the bland pale figure in a biology text. In a flash whose nerve is typical of Edson, we are swept upward, toward stars; "the largest view" dreams the speaker—all this also classic Edson, *right now*, in present tense's immediate warp—until consciousness shrinks and stars are again "only dots" of suns long ago burned out, "leaving only a long wistful string of light." So much for man-made knowledge, rarely the right kind to feed what should be fed. "And I wonder what this has to do with me or the world I attempt to live in," the speaker mourns in phrasing that has become a litany of exhaustion, this motor running down, this body slowly decomposing disguised as a poem.

It is the darkness of prose, its inherent human sense of time, finite and thus tragic, working against the permanent stance of poetry, that makes the prose poem such an unstable, disquieting form. This is Edson's own distinction in his essay "The Prose Poem in America" and if it is true, these two elements are emphatically separate and desperately joined in this poem. What diminishes through prose in the first three paragraphs is moored at either end by an image inexplicable and visionary and poetic: more than can be explained by our conscious examination, less than what will comfort. Now, however, we are coming off summary into the speaker's sometimes lyric, more often wooden rendition of a pointless search. "So I give up astronomy," he says in almost shocking understatement. This is the poem's lowest point, long past the perished stars, a moment borrowed poignantly from their "wistful string of light." Here Edson stops, opens up the page by dropping down two full spaces, forcing silence upon us that reassures, if only briefly.

These pauses in Edson's work are extraordinary in themselves for they are not, as might be argued, mere patience until we get the joke and laugh out loud. Nor are they signals of a dead end in thought, a hesitation while the poet reinvents the world elsewhere. They are, I think, nothing at all, a stunned flight over the plain white page, the blank landscape between synapses. It is as if we are *out* of the poem but not long enough to regain our personal, humdrum intelligence. Nor have we time enough to recollect what Edson has done to us so far; we are still in the poem, trapped by the initial trance. I suspect this is a way to slow us down—Edson's prose poems are, by his own decree, small things—and the pause forces prose's finite motion into poetry's longer view. He is granting equal time to what remains unsaid, something he also suggests by ellipses. Here is the real weight of things, only a part of which rises sufficiently into consciousness to become actual words. The break in the prose allows structural agility as well; the reader is thrown back upon one of the technical resources of poetry, the stanza, and its remarkable ability to pool thought. Between two pools, then, we are hushed and, in this poem at least, allowed to know in ourselves the emptiness that opens at the speaker's admission that he's passed stars into the largest, most wistful view.

As in folk or fairy tale, which Edson's inventions resemble, when the main character reaches the limit of his will, something almost supernatural rises and takes control, wheeling circumstances for good or ill beyond the poor muscle or imagination of human beings. The speaker in "My Head" has, it is true, given up, has exchanged ambition for, well, nothing at all it seems. We could be approaching a kind of freedom in such a position, knowledge that levels everything so we might see, at last, what is.

"I come here now," says the speaker, "into this street, looking up at my head lying half asleep on a windowsill. . . . " The vision, recurring at this moment with so much time and desire drained away, is a wholly different phenomenon. The speaker is no longer *in* time, no longer on his way to anyplace, no longer after meaning in its immensity. "I come here now." There is that head again—*his* head—blinking, lying half asleep, the same one on the same windowsill. Things finally are and they remain, refusing our shallow plans for them. This is the almost unbearable bone of things. Here Edson works courage and modesty again, refusing us the usual claptrap of meaning, only eking out the physical fact, the head now "totally relaxed in the way men become when they have lost all hope."

So we return, as seems right somehow, to give homage to the image itself, grown even odder, darker. The poem ends both like and unlike it began: a head—as the classic Zen utterance might have it— and now it is still a head. We disappear back into ordinary life, carrying off this head in our own heads (a thought that might amuse Edson) as if this outrageous smoking, blinking, disembodied creature were the spoils of a distant nightmare. And we—like the speaker who, in turn, seems like some pagan worshipper torn between awe and sympathy, disgust and compassion—can't bury the thing, can't get it out of our minds. We're stuck.

Edson's work, in short, is that memorable. There is no other poet in America like him, which is surprising news, really, at a time when critics and less finely honed readers complain unto cacophony about the look-alike poem, the so-called workshop poem, the "McPoem," as Donald Hall would have it. Amid the squabble, Edson listens for this other maddening, matter-of-fact world, a place, one suspects, of real furniture and weather whose people move about to supper and back quite without our knowledge. Occasionally, scenes are thrown off in isolate flights and Edson writes them down: bits of things, some more complete than others, but these puzzling inhabitants do not flinch under his scrutiny. Of course our uneasiness is inevitable; we laugh in self-defense. That head on the windowsill, blinking, smoking cigarettes, is not going anywhere. No resolution in the poem will usher out the thing gracefully into the oblivion of final meaning.

By turns we are troubled, then lulled by such a monstrous, indifferent peace.

Melancholy Inside Families

I keep a blue bottle.
Inside it an ear and a portrait.
When the night dominates
the feathers of the owl,
when the hoarse cherry tree
rips out its lips and makes menacing gestures
with rinds which the ocean wind often perforates—
then I know that there are immense expanses hidden from us,
quartz in slugs,
ooze,
blue waters for a battle,
much silence, many ore-veins
of withdrawals and camphor,
fallen things, medallions, kindnesses,
parachutes, kisses.

It is only the passage from one day to another,
a single bottle moving over the seas,
and a dining room where roses arrive,
a dining room deserted
as a fish-bone; I am speaking of
a smashed cup, a curtain, at the end
of a deserted room through which a river passes
dragging along the stones. It is a house
set on the foundations of the rain,
a house of two floors with the required number of windows,
and climbing vines faithful in every particular.

I walk through afternoons, I arrive
full of mud and death,
dragging along the earth and its roots,
and its indistinct stomach in which corpses
are sleeping with wheat,
metals, and pushed-over elephants.

But above all there is a terrifying,
a terrifying deserted dining room,
with its broken olive oil cruets,
and vinegar running under its chairs,
one ray of moonlight tied down,
something dark, and I look
for a comparison inside myself:
perhaps it is a grocery store surrounded by the sea
and torn clothing from which sea water is dripping.

It is only a deserted dining room,
and around it there are expanses,
sunken factories, pieces of timber
which I alone know,
because I am sad, and because I travel,
and I know the earth, and I am sad.

—Pablo Neruda

THE SHAPE OF HIS MELANCHOLY

"I keep a blue bottle," Neruda begins, then stops. Or rather *Conservo un frasco azul*, he says, idling on the line break a half breath or two. So we're launched with a simplicity that is misleading into "Melancholy Inside Families," this great disconcerting piece that reduces nothing, a thing more like a sponge than a poem. Unlike the English first line, which translators Robert Bly and James Wright end-stop calmly and dramatically with a period, Neruda's line is only the beginning of one long sentence that will thread itself down the stanza, bit by rushing bit, to bring us the darkened owl or the cherry tree's "menacing gestures," on and on, a roaring jumble of detail and circumstance. *Roaring* as in Whitman. *Jumble* as in dream, though slowed mid-chant by whisper: "There are immense expanses hidden from us." So these piecemeal things, cast in melancholy and wildly out of context, suggest more disturbing shapes.

One reason it's impossible to get tired of Neruda has to do with this outrageous reach, grotesque and lovely by turns, earthy and weird and exact. One stanza in and already we're deep in slugs and ooze, deranged cherry trees, withdrawals, kisses. The other reason is that hard against this unruly, welcoming passion is humility. The world is weighted by that. One *hears* this double vision; it's in the sound, the pace really, even in translation. The rangy sentence turns early to litany, a shifting backdrop that both belies and shores up the stopped, elegant statement buried in it, that "so much is hidden from us." Past lyric, in a near visionary descent, the speeding imagery mimes ecstasy and revelation and beyond that to a point where everything empties again.

I think Neruda most trusted that point. The rest of the piece grows right out of it. It's in the human scale of his beginning again in stanza two with another modest statement: "only the passage from one day to another." It's in the second bottle there, this one "moving over the seas" thus animating the poem, turning it into journey. Such loss gives way to the central image, the abandoned dining room, its decay of romantic, even mythic proportions, an example of what Neruda himself called his "funereal imagination."

Spooky probably isn't the right word. *Nightmare* is closer, though there is jewel-like comfort in the vines the poet includes and even in the fact that it is a dining room that echoes here, once a place of warmth and nourishment. Neruda's camera work gives grandeur to the desolate scene, great intimacy too as it underscores the unearthly feel and multiplies longing. First the flash of sea, made endless by its plural form, and then the slow, sudden room itself, a zoom-lens flash to bare detail: smashed cup and curtain, the place flooded, rain and more rain unto the very foundation. Then the wide pan out and up to take the whole house, two floors of it, and the final rest on windows and vines, undisturbed.

No one lives here. So there is heartbreak. Solitude and melancholy, already the most intricate embroidery in the poem, deepen color to a stain. One cannot lift one's eyes from the sea-drugged dining room. It fascinates the way ruins always do—the richly *made* thing broken down by the repeated violence of storm and water and wind, shapes that may well suggest but finally overwhelm any human focus. Thus the quiet of another stanza break and the shift to a more chilling litany, nothing like quartz and kindnesses, this time earth itself pulled out by the roots, elephants cut down, corpses, the speaker himself "full of mud and death."

Is it ever possible to know what poems cost? Neruda wrote this piece sometime in his late twenties, toward the end of his various government assignments in the Far East, where he felt profoundly isolated from the resident cultures. Years later, remembering those places, the poet saw himself young, wandering about miserably alone, neither understanding much nor understood. But biographical fact is mere shadow on the page. Not much is narrative here; all is too interior. That's perhaps what keeps us reading Neruda, his direct way to what is felt but barely explainable, past the need for exposition or summary. There is no clarity like his, disembodied imagery notwithstanding. No sorrow like his dirgelike repetitions of detail, no innocence darker than the questions he has the sweetness to ask, ones that take us back to what led us to poetry in the first place.

The penultimate stanza is to me the major movement of the poem, a great wheel coming round again. It's a replay on the dining room, the same "terrifying deserted dining room," but its weight here is as large as its new particulars are small and beautifully figured. We see the broken cruets now, vinegar making a river under the chairs. Then out of nowhere, "one ray of moonlight tied down." (I say the milky Spanish too: *un rayo detenido de la luna*.) "Something dark," he adds. And finally, the defining point for this poet—perhaps for all poetry worth the name—"I look / for a comparison inside myself. . . ."

One can't make too much of this astonishing turn inward. It's not simply Neruda's metaphor as he reaches twice, both times brilliantly, for some image to explain himself to himself—the "grocery store surrounded by the sea" or that "torn clothing from which sea water is dripping." It's the gesture itself that rouses, Neruda's willingness to step back and *not know* how any of this equals or adds up—shattered glass, vinegar and moonlight, this gorgeous misery not something *other* to be taken in and understood but something already there darkening the mind, never to be untangled. The moment is subterranean in another way. Rhetoric's polish and finish dropped, we are witness to the actual making in such a phrase, that humble, often frightening split-second of nowhere and nothing where all one has is the looking. *A comparison inside myself*—as if we could ever know, but where else does great poetry come from?

There is music like this, composers who work a frail, brave moment against an overpowering sweep of sound. Neruda's expanse now takes every broken thing out to sea and sadness, "sunken factories, pieces of timber." Out that far, one hears it—the human heartbeat, tentative, remarkable.

Frau Bauman, Frau Schmidt, and Frau Schwartze

Gone the three ancient ladies
Who creaked on the greenhouse ladders,
Reaching up white strings
to wind, to wind
The sweet-pea tendrils, the smilax,
Nasturtiums, the climbing
Roses, to straighten
Carnations, red
Chrysanthemums; the stiff
Stems, jointed like corn,
They tied and tucked,—
These nurses of nobody else.
Quicker than birds, they dipped
Up and sifted the dirt;
They sprinkled and shook;
They stood astride pipes,
Their skirts billowing out wide into tents,
Their hands twinkling with wet;
Like witches they flew along rows
Keeping creation at ease;
With a tendril for needle
They sewed up the air with a stem;
They teased out the seed that the cold kept asleep,—
All the coils, loops, and whorls.
They trellised the sun; they plotted for more than themselves.

I remember how they picked me up, a spindly kid,
Pinching and poking my thin ribs

Till I lay in their laps, laughing,
Weak as a whiffet;
Now, when I'm alone and cold in my bed,
They still hover over me,
These ancient leathery crones,
With their bandannas stiffened with sweat,
And their thorn-bitten wrists,
And their snuff-laden breath blowing lightly over me in my first sleep.

—Theodore Roethke

Three Spirits

About twenty years ago, I heard a story. And whether it's the true or should-be-true variety may not matter. But Robert Lowell had thrown a party; Roethke was his houseguest. Later, all the revelers having gone home to bed, Lowell was holding forth on this one and that one, the usual party postmortem, stopping, in particular, to point out someone as his "best friend." To which Roethke, large and sad and half-lost by that hour to good drink, is said to have said quietly to Lowell: you're *my* best friend.

I'm still inordinately touched by this anecdote. Roethke's sweetness, his bewildering lack of self-consciousness and embarrassment works disarmingly against the way the elegant Lowell must have surely felt awkward all of a sudden. But other things are carried too— Roethke's edge of self-pity, for instance, disconcertingly near the easy, the sentimental, a peculiarly apt illustration of his much loved and suspect line, "We think by feeling, / What is there to know?" I knew something turned in me nevertheless and won me over. Irony has its pleasures when you're twenty-five. But Roethke, he was downright corny in such a moment, putting himself out there anyway.

I like that *anyway* about him. In this he's one of the most American of twentieth-century poets: expansive, passionately accurate about detail, especially natural detail; secret, sometimes sloppy, reverent, maybe too close for his own good to the heart. He is also one of our most daring (his probably the best ear going), risking not merely ornamental change but real change, from the abstract verities of his first book through the serious grounding of his second—with its so-called greenhouse poems—past that into a disturbing, near-wacko ranging toward singsong rhythms and childish diction, into, finally, the long meditative poems, true wonders of human discovery. Stroked as he was for his first book, *Open House*, he could have easily paid in full and bought that farm—its formal, distant grace—and farmed it for a lifetime. He didn't.

What's forever interesting to me is *how* he didn't, how—because of what?—his second book, *The Lost Son*, arrived. Here's where Michigan comes in, his what must have been, in fact, a rather difficult childhood, son of stolid no-nonsense immigrants (as in "My mother's countenance / could not unfrown itself"), who ran what they considered one of the best nurseries in the Midwest. Still, it was "a wonderful place for a child to grow up," he has written as though in cahoots with the region's PR people, going on to count specific treasures—"twenty-five acres under glass" and farther out, the last stand of virgin timber in the Saginaw Valley, its herons, muskrats, frogs. But the famous greenhouses of that book? "They were to me, I realize now," he told the BBC, "both heaven and hell, a kind of tropics created in the savage climate of Michigan, where austere German-Americans turned their love of order and their terrifying efficiency into something truly beautiful."

Poems, too, are built of heaven and hell, the earth *as is* and under glass, though Roethke's world is forever in that greenhouse shadow, decay there and danger, certainly death, though beauty, it's the thing beyond all doubt. His major life-luck was probably finding that his own accidental place and time made directly for poems, large and close as an ordinary or awful day of childhood. He takes us straight to that place. He shows us something.

Memorable poetry has this way of orbiting the beginning of things to bring on darkness and thus one's first awareness of pattern, ancient cycle, universal turn. "Frau Bauman, Frau Schmidt, and Frau Schwartze" ends the first section of *The Lost Son*, and on the face of it, the poem is elegy, three old greenhouse workers of his father's whom Roethke returns to life, and so praises them. We witness, it seems, everything they ever did or imagined doing—their winding the sweet-pea tendrils, straightening carnations, tying and tucking, dipping, sifting, sprinkling, sewing, teasing out "the seed that the cold kept asleep." The whole first stanza is a busy, lush assemblage of unending duties, the intricate clockwork of the greenhouse in motion before us, quickened by the shortened lines, enjambment making turns both urgent and graceful. Roethke's eye for the right detail brings an almost surreal focus on many things, stems "jointed like corn," or the way these women draw out their silent charges using "a tendril for needle," sewing up the air. It's the view of a child really, a child amazed as an adult might be, looking past the greenhouse ladders to their superhuman handiwork, past their "skirts billowing out wide into tents." Finally, by the stanza's end, one's squinting hard to see that high. "They trellised the sun," the poet tells us. And of their generosity, "they plotted for more than themselves."

Roethke liked to say, quoting Yeats, that "we go from exhaustion to exhaustion." In life and perhaps in any writing too. But immortal now through elegy, these women never tire. The second, final stanza goes abruptly another way. Out of the very public sweep of stanza one, everything goes private, Roethke's favorite way of moving. These focused, workaday women poke and tickle the "spindly kid" the speaker dreams he was. And he laughs too much, "weak as a whiffet." I love this layer, its release against the solid bramble of so much work, the previous climbing, tying, sprinkling, tucking. This other, warmer side is play, and spirit—three spirits, to be exact. In the next line or two, they are invoked like that. They hover now; all's hushed, interior. They guard the speaker, who's grown and recalls what's least romantic in them, these "leathery crones," their "bandannas stiffened with sweat," their "thorn-bitten wrists." Yet even these bits of fact bring, if not peace, at least a kind of consolation. I like to say out loud that fierce, three-stressed phrase *thorn-bitten wrists*, moved by the zoom lens closeness of those hands, by the history of pain and labor in the scratches. The poet honors the essence of those women when he honors that, as well as something larger. Dark and light, heaven and hell in some hopeless mix.

Epithalamion

Hark, hearer, hear what I do; lend a thought now, make believe
We are leafwhelmed somewhere with the hood
Of some branchy bunchy bushybowered wood,
Southern dene or Lancashire chough or Devon cleave,
That leans along the loins of hills, where a candycoloured, where a
    gluegold-brown
Marbled river, boisterously beautiful, between
Roots and rocks, is danced and dandled, all in froth and
    waterblowballs, down.
We are there, when we hear a shout
That the hanging honeysuck, the dogeared hazels in the cover
Makes dither, makes hover
And the riot of a rout
Of, it must be, boys from the town
Bathing: it is summer's sovereign good.

By there comes a listless stranger: beckoned by the noise
He drops toward the river: unseen
Sees the bevy of them, how the boys
With dare and with downdolphinry and bellbright bodies huddling out,
Are earthworld, airworld, waterworld thorough hurled, all by turn and
    turn about.

This garland of their gambols flashes in his breast
Into such a sudden zest
Of summertime joys
That he hies to a pool neighbouring; sees it is the best
There; sweetest, freshest, shadowiest;

Fairyland; silk-beech, scrolled ash, packed sycamore, wild
wychelm, hornbeam fretty overstood
By. Rafts and rafts of flake-leaves light, dealt so, painted on the air,
Hang as still as hawk or hawkmoth, as the stars or as the angles there,
Like the thing that never knew the earth, never off roots
Rose. Here he feasts: lovely all is! No more: off with—down he dings
His bleachèd both and woolwoven wear:
Careless these in coloured wisp
All lie tumbled-to; then with loop-locks
Forward falling, forehead frowning, lips crisp
Over finger-teasing task, his twiny boots
Fast he opens, last he offwrings
Till walk the world he can with bare his feet
And come where lies a coffer, burly all of blocks
Built of chancequarrièd, selfquainèd rocks
And the water warbles over into, filleted with glassy grassy quicksilvery
    shivès and shoots
And with heavenfallen freshness down from moorland still brims,
Dark or daylight on and on. Here he will then, here he will the fleet
Flinty kindcold element let break across his limbs
Long. Where we leave him, froliclavish, while he looks about laughs,
    swims.

Enough now; since the sacred matter that I mean
I should be wronging longer leaving it to float
Upon this only gambolling and echoing-of-earth note—
What is . . . the delightful dene?
Wedlock. What is water? Spousal love.

        . . . .

        . . . .

Father, mother, brothers, sisters, friends
Into fairy trees, wild flowers, wood ferns
Rankèd round the bower

        . . . .

—Gerard Manley Hopkins

Becoming "Epithalamion"

First off, there's its fragmenthood to cherish, watching this poem, this epithalamion, rise and float and fail, not yet—never—caught in any final certainty. "It has some bright lines in it," Hopkins admitted in a rare show of pleasure to his friend and first editor, Robert Bridges, "but I could not get it down." The longing's there, as in all of Hopkins, stretching toward the largest mystery. But "Epithalamion" is a curiously secular piece. It's incomplete, a thing hurried and left; its stall and starts are mortal. Like our human grasp of anything, the poem goes as far as exhaustion goes, or confusion or boredom, until the fine simple nerve it takes to write at all balks then stops unto the stubborn ellipsis.

But we have the giant lucky mess of it. Bridges, naturally, complained: full of "disorder" and "erasures" and "corrections," this draft scribbled on "Royal University of Ireland" candidates' paper, written, he suggests, while Hopkins sat in some dim light administering an exam. One of the last poems he would write, it followed the "terrible sonnets," their "fell of dark," their "cliffs of fall" by three years, a kind of gift, cool relief, this thing planned as a gift to Hopkins's brother Everard and his bride, Amy Sichel. Two things: trance and timidity. These cross angles keep the poem buoyed up and turning on itself like the water it describes.

The crucial thing is trance, though we enter it distantly through rhetoric and only by miming the poet's own deep wish to imagine.

"Hark, hearer, hear what I do; lend a thought now, make believe / We are leafwhelmed somewhere. . . . " Before us opens the "branchy bunchy bushybowered wood," its river "gluegold-brown" and "boisterously beautiful" and so much more, the long layering line after line—one sentence!—of it. Writing richly, so richly in fact it nearly parodies his own high ecstatic style elsewhere, Hopkins seems to cut nothing of the vision. Perhaps this counts: he had just taken up sketching seriously again, mostly woods, and running brooks after a lapse of several years. Still, this is a draft. Which is to say that some one hundred years later, we are close to the moment of initial *seeing*, that first necessary excess. In this breathless expanse, the view flashing aerial (this dene that "leans along the loins of hills") and close up (this river that "is danced and dandled, all in froth and waterblowballs"), Hopkins is all courage, his tentative "make believe" of the start swamped, made true by the triumphant declarative, "We are there. . . . " And we are. Proof: "We hear a shout" in the woods, and can do nothing but follow it.

This is an exacting moment and itself mimics the mind clicking out of its natural blur, into focus. Boys there in "the hanging honeysuck, the dogeared hazels," boys, a dizzy human wealth. Hopkins's double take is in the syntax itself, something he apparently borrowed from Welsh verse, the *tor ymadrodd*, the so-called "interjected absolute." "And the riot of a rout / Of, it must be, boys from town / Bathing," he writes, seems to find again, suddenly, even as we read it . . . *it must be. . . .* That stepping back! Much has been said about movement in Hopkins's poems, their free-fall feel, their high-wire muscle. But against such rapid turn and counterturn is dramatic stillness, a kind of urgent languor. It's through such stillness—*it must be*—that wonder enters.

Then abruptly, there's another level to his reverie. A character, a "listless stranger," comes unseen upon the boys exactly as we have. We who've watched the boys now watch him. It's a commanding shift, and through it silence, the attention *to* silence, deepens and grows complex. Of course, the boys only get louder, more specific and radiant in their antics, full of "dare" and "downdolphinry," their "bellbright bodies huddling out / Are earthworld, airworld, waterworld thorough hurled, all by turn and turn about." In another mood, Hopkins might have stopped the piece right here, this high split-second the thing that ends and overwhelms, his favorite way of closure. But the boys are merely the start; the real heat is yet to come. We're in that far; we're lost, enchanted maybe—to be nineteenth century about it—and the stranger, not so listless now, is fully changed and charged by the sight of such joy.

What gets me is the trees in this transition. The stranger, in finding his own separate "neighbouring" pool, finds it the "sweetest, freshest, shadowiest" ringed about as it is with "silk-beech, scrolled ash, packed sycamore, wild / wychelm, hornbeam. . . ." Here is privacy, more, here's solitude; the depth of shade measures the intensity of the vision. "Here he feasts," Hopkins tells us, "lovely all is!" In such happiness, the most peculiar happens, peculiar, that is, for Hopkins, good Jesuit, *a man takes off his clothes.* Now it's our turn at the *tor ymadrodd*, stepping back, *it must be.* But how precise the poet is, no timidity, no hesitation: " . . . down he dings / His bleachèd both and woolwoven wear. . . ." Hopkins is careful to give us the final fumbling at the "twiny boots," the "lips crisp / Over finger-teasing task" until the stranger can "walk the world" toward water, its "glassy grassy quicksilvery shivès and shoots. . . ."

It's as if we sleepwalk, summoned by the "heavenfallen freshness" of the pool. So deep is this dream that some might say Hopkins has in fact gotten it wrong, the shoes going last, a funny inverse of the million times we've taken off our clothes. But around us, woods, their danger a large measure of their flickering beauty. For generations, we've been this careful—"the soil / Is bare now, nor can foot feel, being shod," Hopkins wrote in lament years earlier. All's so precariously made, but in the final spellbound rush—boots coming off at last, everything exposed—we have that slip into being, the shift from watcher to the one watched, to the one who no longer gives a damn but simply jumps in. It is, I think, an extraordinary moment in a lifetime of work. The water that draws the stranger, that "flinty kindcold element" breaks through all reserve. "We leave him," Hopkins tells us, almost back to his rhetorical overvoice, "froliclavish, while he looks about laughs, swims."

How the poet wakes then, maybe shaking his head—it's right in the text. "Enough now," Hopkins says as though to an unruly child, "since the sacred matter that I mean / I should be wronging longer leaving it to float / Upon this only gambolling and echoing-of-earth note—" In the long naysaying beauty of that sentence, he's nearly set adrift again, purpose waylaid by the charm of recollection.

"An epithalamion on my brother's wedding," he called this painterly fragment—fitting for a brother who actually was a professional artist—and the last section is Hopkins's visible struggle back to that clear-eyed thesis. He hesitates, though all business now. "What is . . . the delightful dene? Wedlock," he intones as if, finally, we've reached the point. "What is water? Spousal love." One feels the drop and press of duty in these questions; albeit awkward, it's endearing, this turning back deliberately, away from dream. But is such an equation really so much the point? Two lines are missing. Bridges called them "disconnected" and simply trashed them. We stare instead at two rows of ellipses as if their pause could tell us something. Elsewhere, the poet is busy, locking himself into overdrive. Wedding? Of course, the wedding. And now the silliest scene unfolds, the entire family set to glitter "rankèd round the bower," parents, siblings, friends slipping into "fairy trees, wild flowers, wood ferns. . . . "

I don't doubt Hopkins's earnestness; it's just that I've never known what to make of this shift to Victorian pop, this leap into the warm nubbies of another age. Are we to believe then, that the whole brilliantly wrought vision of boys and whatever listless stranger, this epiphany really, is merely conceit, a device to shoulder up one side of metaphor? "I could not get it done," Hopkins wrote to Bridges, giving up. His reluctance to work these two strands together is itself revealing.

But of what? Surely in Hopkins's standstill, one remembers things too bone-close, too strange for words at all. It's in that depth of shade, those trees, that stranger's rare fever that would have us strip down every trace of the human-made world to be engulfed and buoyed up by water. For a poem supposedly about union, the central heat is solitude, less about the self than about its letting go. For Hopkins is not reacting, not making sense of circumstance. Nor is he the poet simply pleased to watch his own starry mind at work. He's made something and put it out there and he can't explain. Imagination here is more than palpable; it is place. That's the poetry in this poem. That's its lucid, sea-green light.

Field and Forest

When you look down from the airplane you see lines,
Roads, ruts, braided into a net or web—
Where people go, what people do: the ways of life.

Heaven says to the farmer: "What's your field?"
And he answers: "Farming," with a field,
Or: "Dairy-farming," with a herd of cows.
They seem a boy's toy cows, seen from this high.

Seen from this high,
The fields have a terrible monotony.

But between the lighter patches there are dark ones.
A farmer is separated from a farmer
By what farmers have in common: forests,
Those dark things—what the fields were to begin with.
At night a fox comes out of the forest, eats his chickens.
At night the deer come out of the forest, eats his crops.

If he could he'd make farm out of all the forest,
But it isn't worth it: some of it's marsh, some rocks,
There are things there you couldn't get rid of
With a bulldozer, even—not with dynamite.
Besides, he likes it. He had a cave there, as a boy;
He hunts there now. It's a waste of land,
But it would be a waste of time, a waste of money,
To make it into anything but what it is.

At night, from the airplane, all you see is lights,
A few lights, the lights of houses, headlights,
And darkness. Somewhere below, beside a light,
The farmer, naked, takes out his false teeth:
He doesn't eat now. Takes off his spectacles:
He doesn't see now. Shuts his eyes.
If he were able to he'd shut his ears,
And as it is, he doesn't hear with them.
Plainly, he's taken out his tongue: he doesn't talk.
His arms and legs: at least, he doesn't move them.
They are knotted together, curled up, like a child's.
And after he has taken off the thoughts
It has taken him his life to learn,
He takes off, last of all, the world.

When you take off everything what's left? A wish,
A blind wish; and yet the wish isn't blind,
What the wish wants to see, it sees.

There in the middle of the forest is the cave
And there, curled up inside it, is the fox.

He stands looking at it.
Around him the fields are sleeping: the fields dream.
At night there are no more farmers, no more farms.
At night the fields dream, the fields *are* the forest.
The boy stands looking at the fox
As if, if he looked long enough—

                                    he looks at it.
Or is it the fox that's looking at the boy?
The trees can't tell the two of them apart.

—Randall Jarrell

Rhetoric and Mystery

Some poems seem profoundly, willfully plain. Still, these efficient hosts, eventually bored by the party, might usher us out past the church, past the large showy houses that look like cakes, into the blank countryside of a listless month, November maybe. Little is said really and what's said is repeated, moving with reserve and overlap toward the reason of the trip. No digression. Nothing ornate, airy, playful: this *seems* so ordinary. When everything stops, just above the treeline, we are nodded to the old quarry abandoned for years, spread out before us like some heroic aftermath, cliffs that startle by color, size, but mainly now by a massive repetitive uselessness. This presence, kept until now, might be what the poem exhausts itself to know, this private thing that has no reason but beauty or our astonishment before it. I'm imagining Randall Jarrell writing "Field and Forest" and I imagine it caught him off guard. In spite of its rhetorical current and rise, something unpredictable swamps the journey by the end, something mute and close. Jarrell lets it take over, uncharacteristically lets the poem steer itself.

All begins coolly enough in an airplane, higher than we normally conceive of things. That the country below keeps its "terrible monotony" or reminds us of something it never actually is close up—roads become webs and nets, cows "toy cows"—is more than a visual trick; it settles us into our seats, makes us believe we are, in fact, in air. From this distance, seeing what appears to be the whole thing, we can judge, dismember, condescend with impunity. After all, no one's watching us. We're alone here, the perspective abstract and set by category—people and their "ways of life," their "fields"—while the airplane hums its own complex order. Immediately, then, we're in the grip of Jarrell's familiar authority: his assumption of audience, his careful definition. *He knows things.* We sit back, waiting for his offhand intellectual delight or anguish, waiting, that is, until the jolt. One word—"but"—opens that heavy door. "But," the poet warns, "between the lighter patches there are dark ones."

This line is a second take. Though we still feel that guarded rhetorical momentum, there *is* darkness now amid the "lighter patches," and cleverly Jarrell tells us that "a farmer is separated from a farmer / By what farmers have in common: forests," a cleverness which turns on itself as Frost's sometimes does, in deadpan, deliberate measure. What I value next is the undercut, abrupt and childlike, spoken right now. "Forests," Jarrell declares, "those dark things—what the fields were to begin with." One hears earnest impatience in the voice. "Those dark things . . . " *You* know. And then, belied by an encyclopedic calm, come the dangerous facts of such woods: foxes emerge and eat chickens; deer move out and destroy crops. Always "at night" when the universe quiets, out of control.

By now we are helplessly descending, launched from the plane completely, inventing a single owner, a farmer and his lifetime of sweat and silence in these fields. The farmer thinks like a farmer, with practicality; he is not romanticized. Sure the guy would like to farm all this knotty worthless woods. Ways exist; they don't work. "There are things there you couldn't get rid of / With a bulldozer, even—not with dynamite," we hear or, rather, overhear, for this is the sort of remark that comes drifting above the spring seed bins in hardware stores, this injunction that layers like a virus, hitting the body by degrees, in various calculations of meaning. We know by its weight that here is some major artery of the poem. But Jarrell is offhand, still in-character. "Besides," the poet tells us of the farmer, "he likes it. He had a cave there, as a boy," as if an apologist were needed for this image that cuts back to our first longing for shelter and solitude, for a place before history or manners or grown-up routine. It would be a waste, the voice continues with purposeful bravado and purposefully beside the point, a waste of land, time, money to make it "anything but what it is." *What it is.* We've arrived at a primal something. But what? One feels a chill, a suspension. The idea at hand is that large.

Instead, Jarrell's off target, not ready. He shifts back, barely, breaking stanza, back to observation from the high confines of the plane. He chants the hard details. Up here, one sees "lights / a few lights, the lights of houses, headlights, / And darkness." Mostly, of course, darkness. Which is to say, one sees nothing at all. This is dream. We are aloft over fields that may or may not be fields anymore. We lose hold of proof. There is memory certainly, and Jarrell drifts in its earnest if inexact digressions. Darkness, however, is indifferent; it levels and forgets, and one feels the poet stalling in these lines, a swimmer coming up in a passion for common air, a traveler lulled by the plane's bright efficiency, gearing up. Before invention took us as far as the cave. How willing is Jarrell now to let imagination fall as darkness falls, as a seed falls windward? If he is stalling—I sense he must be— then some dangerous turn is imminent.

"Somewhere below," the poet gropes, "beside a light"—of course, his eye's at the keyhole!—"the farmer, naked, takes out his false teeth." Not any farmer, *the* farmer—of the cave, of the ominous tangle of field and forest. In a second, all is aging. The farmer's instantly old, alone for years. And the listing that follows, echo of grandparent after grandparent witnessing to ailments like serious collectors at their stamps, buries us with detail: tooth and eye, ear and tongue, all diminished. "He doesn't move them." Arms and legs. "They are knotted together, curled up, like a child's."

Envision this room then, and the gradual, almost matter-of-fact reduction of body. The poet, however, goes further. "And after he has taken off the thoughts / It has taken him his life to learn, / He takes off, last of all, the world." Jarrell ends the stanza with extraordinary poise: *the world*—which takes a lifetime to enter. Beyond exhaustion now, beyond gratitude even, one slips out easily, the way at bedside one slips out of a shirt too big, too worn, too familiar. In turn, a stanza break consoles us just when we need it, silence here, witness to the dark expanse within the farmer, back to middle age, to youth, to boyhood. We are down in this descent to "what's left," this thing that can't be altered in us. "A wish," Jarrell insists, that is blind and not so blind because what it "wants to see, it sees."

At this point, Jarrell is past philosophy too, narrowing like some heat-sensitive device toward the heart of the vision, off explanation, onto pure image. There is the forest and there, inside it, is the cave. Smaller, as in some folktale riddle, is the fox of course, curled up in the cave, seemingly asleep. "He," Jarrell tells us simply, "stands looking at it." *He*—the farmer, with his one wish. How long does it take to be where we want to be? The poet expands to backdrop and foreground, but everything's nearer now. "The fields dream," he tells us. More, "At night . . . the fields *are* the forest." Then in a similar transfer, more remarkable, it's "the boy" looking at the fox in pure attention. "As if," the poet manages, "if he looked long enough—" *As if, as if. . . .* The poet is, unbelievably, out of words.

Jarrell—does he have a choice?—waits here, poised in the near empty length of line. One recovers from mystery slowly, no doubt more slowly than this, but now the speaker is not asking to know anything at all. What began this poem, this need to contain, to distance and simplify, has ended—was anything less predictable?—in this extraordinary moment of speechlessness: night and its dreaming field taken into the body like the oldest elixir. The boy or the fox? Who's looking at whom? Jarrell asks. But even as he asks, he's beyond us, long past this calculation, throwing such small confining dazzlements elsewhere, to trees even.

An Embroidery   *(IV) Swiss Cheese*

(after a lost poem, 1947)

Lost wooden poem,
cows and people wending
downmountain slowly
to wooden homesteads

cows first, the families
following calmly their swaying,
their pausing, their moving ahead in dreamy
constancy.
Children asleep in arms of old men,
healthy pallor of smooth cheeks facing
back to high pastures left for the day,
are borne down as the light
waits to leave.

Upper air glows with motes color of hay,
deep valley darkens.
Lost poem, I know
the cows were fragrant
and sounds were of hooves and feet on earth,
of clumps of good grass torn off, to chew
slowly; and not much talk.
They were returning
to wooden buckets, to lantern-beams
crisp as new straw.

Swiss cheese with black bread,
meadow, wood walls, what

did I do with you, I'm looking
through holes, in cheese, or
pine knotholes, and

who were those peaceful folk, the poem
was twenty years ago, I need it now.

—Denise Levertov

Two Veils

I'm not sure people do this anymore, or not much anyway—
embroidery—though when I was a child, you could still earn a
badge in Girl Scouts with it. That peculiar, willful stitching would
turn up in expected places though always a surprise somehow:
daffodils carefully embedded near the hem of a line-dried, stiffened
pillowcase one was almost too tired to notice, or on the edge of some
handkerchief no one dared use, folded in a perfumed drawer.

That Denise Levertov would launch a modest four-poem series
from real embroideries or perhaps only using that template to frame
her meditations, thus drawing on its delicate, static aura, seems
completely in keeping with the time she came of age. Surely such
handiwork was still valued. Yet already the whole business must
have been tinted with nostalgia, war and then postwar, the surge of
shiny new beginnings everywhere. The act of drawing lightly with
pencil on a small cotton expanse, then taking a needle and its col-
orful thread to follow such design—that took hours, took an eye
comfortable with measure, the stop and start of it, the glint of the
needle vanishing into the underside of cloth and reappearing,
steady, in a burst of red or blue. In a way, the entire idea of embroidery seems a kind of *ars poetica* for Levertov, whose work has
always been, for me at least, soaked in dream but kept absolutely
alert—kept meticulous, one might say—through detail inch by
inch, the pacing managed in part with small and large white spaces,

the way itself disappearing then coming back in the weight of a singular image, dangerous needle piercing the fabric.

Meanwhile, in her actual series "Four Embroideries," Levertov begins and largely stays with *story* or *retold story*, not an overwhelming habit elsewhere in her work. She invokes the old tale "Red Rose and White Rose" in one, then the lesser known "Catherine and Her Destiny" from Andrew Lang's collection that her mother read to her as a child, and, in her third section, the more obscure "Red Snow" drawn from *Parables from Nature*, she tells us in the parenthetical epigraph, first collected by a certain "Mrs. Getty"—Margaret Getty, it turns out, whose book was wildly popular with children or parents *of* those children in the late nineteenth century. These first three "embroideries," their stories told and variously interpreted for us, hold interest, but the poet, as personal speaker with something clearly at stake, does not entirely enter, not yet.

It is the fourth and last part of this series, "Swiss Cheese," where that full entry comes. "After a lost poem, 1947," Levertov writes, again in a parenthetical epigraph, and suddenly with the words "after" and "lost," we're hearing a new kind of telling, self-conscious, fragile, cut with grief or at least with a *looking back* that might draw out such grief. So we're prepared, though one might argue that in this fourth section we're already prepared, working off the three previous sections. Well, that too. Nevertheless, it's the *lost* in that epigraph that makes us hesitate, but we open, then, to this:

> Lost wooden poem,
> cows and people wending
> downmountain slowly
> to wooden homesteads
>
> cows first, the families
> following calmly their swaying,

> their pausing, their moving ahead in dreamy
> constancy.

As clear as this narrative seems, there's a small confusion from the onset. Is this *about* an actual memory, and if so, something seen? Or read of? Perhaps it's the poet just tracing the stitched figures of an old embroidery after all. Beyond that, is it simply the imagery of the "lost" poem that she reconstructs here? And why a "wooden" poem, as she calls it in the first line before describing the descent on the mountain, unless it's a reference to an imagery almost mythic, whole families—old men, children, the cows they care for—coming down after a day's work into twilight and rest.

Perhaps such confusion is deliberate, part of the speaker's sense of the mysterious: How do poems come about, anyway? And what is a poem, the made thing itself? The memory of that making? All the worlds attached to it before coming into being? This questioning, the epigraph insists on it. In that spirit, Levertov chooses to cast these first few lines as fragment, heavy with half-verbs, almost-verbs set in motion by their *ing* form, as if nothing is ever complete and everything immediate; we live to enter and exit midsentence.

Yet the uncertainty of the syntax is balanced by the poet's trademark rock-hard clarity of image. One sees this flash of humanity in a weird, weighted motion, nothing blurred: cows first with "their swaying, / their pausing," and their human owners who follow and presumably share their "dreamy constancy." It's all "downmountain," this movement; Levertov's running together these words faintly mimes the ghostly *kenning*, sweet, dark habit of Old English. It's not exact, this equation, her double word not two nouns fused together but still intriguing—especially given the poem's reversed sequence, "mountain" at first thought, simply *up*, all peak—but here, from the start, it's the other way, a retreat, a surrender in the slow going down. And now, more detail: "Children asleep in arms of old men" and a quick reference back to the hours before, the "high pastures," a phrase thrilling to me, a flatlander, a midwesterner for whom the word *high* will never, in this life, routinely coexist with the lovely sanity of *pasture*. By the end of that sentence—Levertov's first complete one—it's light that enters, light given near-human sensibility in that it "waits to leave."

Undoubtedly, light is a major image throughout Levertov's work. In some ways, hers is a highly moral imagination, its power dependent on primal distinctions and the oldest of imagery that underscores them, but she can be unnervingly subtle. Here, as we move into the third stanza, it's the nonhuman, even the nonanimal world that comes clear in a swift expansive turn. The sweep is on landscape; we see by both detail and summary that the "upper air glows with motes color of hay, / deep valley darkens." So light finds its heavier twin, but by putting *dark* into its verb form, Levertov enlivens it, gives it flight. We see it as it happens.

Thus the sudden shift to direct address. "Lost poem," she writes, "I know. . . . " (Direct address? Maybe, maybe not. But that ambiguity seems delicious to me.) In fact, this leap feels both jarring and inevitable. Where else to go at this point but inward to the past and fully personal after such a vista, the entire valley visible from this height? It's in such simple moves that Levertov's grace is evident, in the quietly ecstatic slips she makes *into* and *out of*, between worlds. Now the lost poem is fully evoked, its specifics more striking—

> Lost poem, I know
> the cows were fragrant
> and sounds were of hooves and feet on earth,
> of clumps of good grass torn off, to chew
> slowly; and not much talk.

In the scent of cows, the sound of both hooves and human feet on the trail, the "clumps of good grass torn off, to chew," Levertov hammers and quickens memory with a monosyllabic run—a characteristic gesture—ending just in time to turn the sentence at its line break—another famous habit—to a more thoughtful speed. "Slowly," she says of the cow's rhythm, the two syllables drawn out, making it so. Still linked by a semicolon, the sentence, but barely, continues—"and not much talk." It's that "not much talk," how it takes us down to nothing but such a nothing! Everything's open after all; one looks *out* at it. In this way, another small expansive moment passes before the rush of real fact, still in downward motion—of the mountain, of the life. "They were returning," she tells us, "to wooden buckets, to lantern-beams / crisp as new straw."

So much for the scene and the remembered scene, a veil on it now, two veils really, the recollection of the lost poem—there *was* such a poem of "cows and people wending / downmountain"—and then the second remembering, a far more complex rendering where children sleep in adult arms, where cows eat slowly and take all the time in the world. In the remaining three stanzas, full of brief litanies and questions, the speaker looking seemingly everywhere "through holes, in cheese, or / pine knotholes" to bring this moment back, I hear a new voice. It's not the certain, smart overvoice of the earlier pieces in this embroidery series but a sound more tentative—"what / did I do with you" and "who were these peaceful folk" worn down to no-longer-questions-at-all, pressed now with a sorrow that changes them to statements we might circle endlessly, never getting to the end of that circling. Finally, the poet is surprisingly direct: "I need it now," she tells us point-blank about the remembered scene or the remembered poem, ending everything in a whisper, past entreaty. It's an utterance to the self against times, perhaps, not so pleasant, years of holding forth and being sure, or not so sure; we only overhear it. Are we also stopped? Yes. And all lost things come surging back.

Forgive me. This is not one of Levertov's finest poems; I certainly do not argue that. It's a genre all by itself, a poem *about* a poem; in this case, the first vanished version apparently written in 1947, this second, I would guess, about 1968, which is to say, a made thing about a made thing and all the lost time and life between. This is the small shock of her "I need it now," that to look back is also to look *right now, here* and feel absence, something that takes us inward to pure air and high places. That Levertov included this fourth embroidery among her poems of conscience in *Relearning the Alphabet* (1970), a collection largely reflecting the angst and struggle of the Vietnam War, makes the piece more poignant, the poet's need for those near mythic "peaceful folk" a greater counterweight.

One last thought. Toward the end of her life, Levertov put together *Tesserae*, a book she called "merely fragments," prose pieces written now and then "between poems." The last of these, "A Lost Poem," mourns another misplaced piece that merged two images she dreamt one night, a richly appointed Florentine cathedral and the piazza of a poor Mexican town. She mentions another poem in passing, this one not surprisingly "about Swiss peasants, men, women and children, returning to their village after a harvest day in the mountain pastures." Of both poems, she writes that if ever found, "will (they) tell me anything more? Anything I have forgotten?" Of the dream-triggered poem and its uneasy confluence, she goes on to say that what remains for her is not the idea that the cathedral could be stripped, its treasures sold off to feed the poor, though that notion "cannot fail to occur." It's just that images persist—the "glimmering . . . pearls" in the cathedral's "darkness of stone"—because of "the deep pleasure that beauty was to those who passed and repassed." And do such arguments bring anything back? One poem, two? Or was it poetry itself she meant?

The End of March

For John Malcolm Brinnin and Bill Read: Duxbury

It was cold and windy, scarcely the day
to take a walk on that long beach.
Everything was withdrawn as far as possible,
indrawn: the tide far out, the ocean shrunken,
seabirds in ones or twos.
The rackety, icy, offshore wind
numbed our faces on one side;
disrupted the formation
of a lone flight of Canada geese;
and blew back the low, inaudible rollers
in upright, steely mist.

The sky was darker than the water
—*it* was the color of mutton-fat jade.
Along the wet sand, in rubber boots, we followed
a track of big dog-prints (so big
they were more like lion-prints). Then we came on
lengths and lengths, endless, of wet white string,
looping up to the tide-line, down to the water,
over and over. Finally, they did end:
a thick white snarl, man-size, awash,
rising on every wave, a sodden ghost,
falling back, sodden, giving up the ghost. . . .
A kite string?—But no kite.

I wanted to get as far as my proto-dream-house,
my crypto-dream-house, that crooked box

set up on pilings, shingled green,
a sort of artichoke of a house, but greener
(boiled with bicarbonate of soda?),
protected from spring tides by a palisade
of—are they railroad ties?
(Many things about this place are dubious.)
I'd like to retire there and do *nothing*,
or nothing much, forever, in two bare rooms:
look through binoculars, read boring books,
old, long, long books, and write down useless notes,
talk to myself, and, foggy days,
watch the droplets slipping, heavy with light.
At night, a *grog à l'américaine*.
I'd blaze it with a kitchen match
and lovely diaphanous blue flame
would waver, doubled in the window.
There must be a stove; there *is* a chimney,
askew, but braced with wires,
and electricity, possibly
—at least, at the back another wire
limply leashes the whole affair
to something off behind the dunes.
A light to read by—perfect! But—impossible.
And that day the wind was much too cold
even to get that far,
and of course the house was boarded up.

On the way back our faces froze on the other side.
The sun came out for just a minute.
For just a minute, set in their bezels of sand,
the drab, damp, scattered stones
were multi-colored,
and all those high enough threw out long shadows,
individual shadows, then pulled them in again.

They could have been teasing the lion sun,
except that now he was behind them
—a sun who'd walked the beach the last low tide,
making those big, majestic paw-prints,
who perhaps had batted a kite out of the sky to play with.

—Elizabeth Bishop

ORIGINAL SHELL

"The End of March," like so much of Elizabeth Bishop, travels well. The poem appeared in the *New Yorker* in 1975. I cut it out and, after her death, took it with me to Taiwan for a couple of years: a map, a kind of message scrawled suddenly, and kept. Only one walk I took ever resembled it at all, but I gladly took that, one glaring morning. After stretches of hot machine-and-concrete-gutted land, my husband and I crossed a small bridge, entered a bamboo thicket. Deep shade, its hazy quiet. Relief enough. But nothing prepared us for the cabin of split bamboo there, the tiny porch, chickens in idle happiness, fruit in a wooden bowl. What a bare and hospitable place. We peered in every window. Absolutely empty! Abandoned? Impossible. Every inch spoke, suggested, sang. We hurried off, feeling marvelous and guilty, savoring each detail of the place as though it were possible to us, lived in for years, loved.

Possible. Even when it is not in hand, no longer tied to words on paper, "The End of March" keeps intact its kernel of sense and solitude, coming forward physically and imaginatively through that strange "artichoke of a house." On the page though, the power of that image increases by careful timing. Two stanzas of annoyances precede it: foul weather, the inexplicable string and footprints, the prosaic stop-start web of italics, parenthesis, comparison, complaint. Not a pretty landscape. What it is, is interesting, withholding more than it offers, inscrutable in spite of any human rush for meaning. What it is, most of all, is possible. This sense of possibility—of *maybe*, nothing sure—is pure Bishop; we enter so many of her poems on that offhand silk. Still, "It was cold and windy, scarcely the day / to take a walk on that long beach," she tells us. Consider yourself warned, I read. So we are reckoned with, not condescended to in the odd invitation. And of course the house, where these two meandering, hard-working stanzas are headed, is not the house-beautiful retreat of the writer but "dubious," a "crooked box"; in short, possible. At once it is ours too: something longing creates, the eccentric dream.

What delights is that eccentricity. "I wanted to get as far as my proto-dream-house, / my crypto-dream-house. . . ." In the half-frozen muddy stupor of the walk, that voice—joking, matter-of-fact—wakes us. Yet what a pathetic, lovely, cartoonish place it points to: shingled greener than the artichoke "(boiled with bicarbonate of soda?)," makeshift, shielded by railroad ties, a chimney "askew . . . braced with wires." A gem of flotsam set adrift against murky seascape. And how careful Bishop is to know it, in busy proprietorship, assuming stove, electricity from a few feeble wires, finding its pilings for us, imagining spring tides. More, right before our eyes, she has moved in for good, her days and nights already planned or, rather, quite rescued from plan. *Nothing*, she emphasizes, to do nothing, "or nothing much, forever, in two bare rooms."

Naturally, Bishop's "nothing" brims with life and humor: books to read, but of a specific nature—old, long, and boring; things to write, but just "useless notes"; conversations, but only the kind of consoling, ranting banter one practices alone. After dark, the splendid moment arrives, lit double against the window, when the final drink is readied, its flame "lovely diaphanous blue." So the house—this unlikely wreck propped up against confusing shoreline—becomes in the deepest sense inhabited, in the most authentic way renewing.

Maybe all poems, in one way or another, redefine shelter. One enters such places and notices things. More important, one enters and closes the door. It was Gaston Bachelard's notion in his *Poetics of Space* that the *house*, as image and fact, begins and ends here: to shield the dreamer, to allow one "to dream in peace," to return us, be the structure palatial or primitive, to that immediate sure sense of "the original shell" and so into well-being, into memory and solace. Solitude surrounds these rooms; however fanciful Bishop's "nothing," her boredom clears the place for private truth. Risk in her poem—the long difficult trek down the unseasonable beach—is stalking something of crucial value: safety.

Safety. How safe are we? She could have turned up a collar, buttoned a higher button, holding forth feverishly on the cutting wind. Instead, with sharp flourish, we are plucked out of the weather into warmth and grace and light—enough "to read by" anyway. Now when I take up this poem, I read for this stanza, hope for its rescue. Here are the confusions of the world. We pass through them. And here, in the shoddy lean-to, is sense. They are a separate music, each quite indifferently drowning out the other. Bishop is no idealist; we are where we are. There is little reason for it, only forbearance before it, or gratitude.

Maybe things go harder, more complex than this. Characteristically, Bishop refuses to leave us glad and alone in our elation and gently, reasonably, leads us, where? Simply *back*. "Perfect! But—impossible." The fact remains that the place can't be owned and never, in spite of Bishop's charmed invention, either day or night spent there. The wind "too cold," the house no doubt "boarded up," the return's small comfort is that now the other side of the face is freezing. Yet as in anything by Elizabeth Bishop, such a deprecating remark should make us suspicious.

In fact, something happens. This is a journey; we hold the map in our hands and it is changed as it is traveled. In a moment, "the drab, damp, scattered stones" assume color and movement into shadow. In a moment, resolution, almost too fantastic—but of course Bishop knows this—takes a playful leap. At once, the artifacts—footprints, string—of an earlier bedevilment are cleared. Nothing's inevitable, not even the darkest going back. Wherever that odd artichoke of a house continues, its single wire bolted so wryly, reluctantly to the world, one goes there to begin.

In the Twentieth Century

My brother died in the twentieth century.
I played hopscotch at twilight in the twentieth century.
The dead gave us whiplash in the twentieth century.

I saw the moon shipwrecked in the twentieth century.
I lived in a country of fireflies in the twentieth century.
The dead wanted us all to themselves in the twentieth century.

My brother died in the twentieth century.
I wasted three years on geometry in the twentieth century.
I shed pints of blood in the twentieth century.

The dead exhausted themselves in the twentieth century.
The dead echoed like hammer-strokes in the twentieth century.
The dead drank fistfuls of rainwater in the twentieth century.

I ate sweet apples in the twentieth century.
I ate my peck of dirt in the twentieth century.
I ate my words in the twentieth century.

My father was ten minutes older than the twentieth century.
He shoveled black coal in pitch dark in the twentieth century.
My brother died in the twentieth century.

My mother watched *Gone with the Wind* thirty-two times in the
    twentieth century.
She sold zucchini and rhubarb in the twentieth century.
I wrote ridiculous poems in the twentieth century.

I was incapable of keeping silent in the twentieth century.
My marriage ended in the twentieth century.
My marriage ended in the twentieth century.

I loved Kawasaki in the twentieth century.
I danced like a sumac tree in the twentieth century.
I prayed to the Son of Man in the twentieth century.

I was anesthetized through most of the twentieth century.
I wrote passionate letters in the twentieth century.
I went to a sensitivity workshop and had my umbrella stolen in the
    twentieth century.

The dead jiggled the change in their pockets in the twentieth century.
There was something very obvious in the twentieth century
I could never see or understand.

It was nearly possible to live in the twentieth century.
The dead knocked on the door of my life in the twentieth century.
Who's there? I said in the twentieth century.

—Tom Andrews

The End of a Century

There are ways to write elegy, indeed, to live it. This is not my wish in thinking about Tom Andrews. What first comes to mind, and keeps coming, is the real story of one of my first meetings with him, years ago now, he and his wife, Carrie, over to supper, and of course, even before coming in the door, Tom found my son's skateboard on the porch. This is anti-elegy. This is merely Tom seizing that skateboard and rushing out to the street with it—Maple Street, with its decidedly downhill slope—shouting back to us, especially to my son then in grade school: Okay! Are you ready? Watch this! And we did. And there was Tom, this poet, this *hemophiliac*, suddenly *upside down*, doing a handstand on that skateboard, grinning broadly nevertheless, whizzing merrily straight down the street. Was anything ever this out-rageous, this oh-my-god? It was Carrie next to me, the only calm one among us, calm unto amused, singing out: Hey you on the skateboard! Do you want to get married?

I tell this story a lot, my favorite glimpse of Tom among the many other, much darker glimpses. It shores up something still vastly open and deep. To place Tom in the company of such danger and joy, to place him again where he once placed himself, is to see him in his own favorite state of *being*, steady and reckless both, in utter contradiction. And that mystery—all of it richly tangled in this poet, this *person*—lives on through the work.

So I want to put my small lens on what I think the most haunting poem in that work, last or next to lastly written. When I say *haunting*, I mean that in all the wistful, scary, beloved ways that come to us. To be haunted for the writer means to be followed, tracked down, in the dim half-light of wonders beyond one's control, all elements passed on to readers by way of this mysterious, wily conduit: the poem itself. So the poem becomes *haunting* and we, in turn, are haunted by it.

I mean, of course, the penultimate poem in the posthumous collected edition, the piece called "In the Twentieth Century." I see this poem as nearly sung—to the self and to others, not just something we overhear, not Yeats's argument with the self as opposed to the world. Which is to say, this poem is an obsessive prayer of sorts but a chant too, a litany, a long stutter of things known and unknown. And so much is here. Formally cast in tercets—that uneven, unstable three-line stanza that nevertheless keeps coming in its orderly way, this poem is a large, concisely woven net of *All Things Tom;* his trademark wit, for instance, moves through the piece like some sweet elastic (his going to a "sensitivity workshop" only to have his umbrella stolen or the fact that his mother watched *Gone with the Wind* not once but thirty-two times). Against this and painfully, lovingly merged, we find more sobering turns, of course the loss of his brother or his own hemophilia ("I shed pints of blood in the twentieth century") but also the dead writ large, back again and again in seemingly numberless ways, simply "the dead"—here an army or a quartet, it hardly matters—these dead who return seven times in the poem to make a litany within a litany in their heroic generality to be and do nevertheless specific, primal things: to drink and echo, to jiggle the change in their pockets, to grow exhausted, to knock at the door.

Always there is this knocking at the door, this drumbeat and return. That's of course the *haunted* part, or part of it. Whitman loved this as sheer method too. The long reach of Tom's lines seems almost a musical quotation in homage to that poet. Whitman's repeats in so many of his poems are famously riveting, a build, a veritable *Bolero* of sound and image. In Tom's hands, it's equally hypnotic—the dead the dead the dead or my marriage ended, my marriage ended or my brother died, my brother died or just the stubborn underscoring— each line!—of time and place, that real time and place now unbelievably lost to all of us who once lived "in the twentieth century" year after year quite thoughtlessly, thank you, we who would live there still if it hadn't turned on us. Now, in Tom's poem, this phrase grounds every whimsy, every grief. Cut to memory. Cut to right now, now all of us thinking *about* that twentieth century. End-stop. End-stop. Every line. Almost every line.

Yet I am never grounded in this poem. I am never at rest. I am never finished. Which is to say, I am always surprised. Partly this is due to the variation quietly burning against the repeated pattern of fact ("in the twentieth century") and static, never-to-be-resolved tears of things (the dead echo and knock, a marriage ends, a brother dies). We get, quite out of nowhere, juxtaposed in the best sense, a further gift— expansive, small, funny, uncertain. It's in the diction, from the high romance of "I saw the moon shipwrecked in the twentieth century" to the willfully plain way the speaker's mother sells "zucchini and rhubarb" in the twentieth century. It keeps coming, this kaleidoscopic shifting, and perfectly clear, each detail self-sufficient: "I wasted three years on geometry in the twentieth century" or "I loved Kawasaki in the twentieth century" or (my father) "shoveled black coal in pitch dark in the twentieth century" or "I ate sweet apples" or—and here Tom's love for the curious solace of self-disparagement rears up—"I wrote ridiculous poems in the twentieth century," though "I was incapable of keeping silent," he tells us later—a fact for which we were grateful "in the twentieth century" and, now, beyond it.

Elsewhere in his work, we find a poet in love with enjambment, that habit of line that resists the sentence's orderly, know-it-all logic, instead, at the break, to hesitate, think again, second-guess in the half-breath it takes to turn and descend to the next line, the next level.

Tom's shape for this litany, to end-stop his lines and thus heighten their authority ("Period. Paragraph," as my mother would say in a grand gesture of finality in arguments I mostly lost), feels new here and carries with it the weight of elegy: this far, no farther, line after line, *this is all I can bear*. That is, until we move toward closure and suddenly Tom's release of that habit feels huge. "There was something very obvious in the twentieth century," he tells us in the penultimate stanza, "I could never see or understand," the words *obvious* and *never see* in passionate, fateful dissonance.

We return, in a show of knowing or almost knowing, to the end-stopped line for the last stanza. And the dead come back and certainly in this dream of time and place, the twentieth century is here once more as refrain to end all three lines in this final tercet. But the press of that "never" seeing, "never understanding" darkens all this. It's a different sort of sepia we feel in the last line that begins with a question. Naturally, a question—no, a joke!—old utterance of bus stops and lunchrooms and playgrounds: knock knock, someone was always blurting out, this demand that asks and opens. Here, because this is Tom Andrews who knew such shade, it's the dead returning to knock on the door, on *this* life, in this twentieth century. And again, *because* it's Tom, we can imagine in that final line his real voice brightly answering in the careful pretense of not-doom: "Who's there? I said in the twentieth century." So we wait. And so this poem never ends.

Worlds Old and New

Indianapolis, early summer. We're somewhere in the middle of Dvořák's Symphony no. 9—"from the new world" he said, as afterthought—finished over a century ago. They're rehearsing all four movements but now it's the slow sad center where rising woodwinds, brass, and timpani give way to the muted strings, a melody, a countermelody, weave upon weave of a thing past sound and far into longing. These one hundred or so musicians are young, mostly in high school, a few in junior high, and a very few even younger than that, a youth orchestra then, the New World Youth Symphony Orchestra, aptly enough. And the sound is full and rich and so much larger than this room. Now their conductor, Susan Kitterman, holds up her hand, gesturing *stop stop*, and the held notes fall like rain, the moment awkward, disorienting, the way one wakes from dream. Everyone looks up. Did you hear that? she says to them. Did you hear how beautiful that is? She looks down at the score for a second then back to her young players. That's why we play music, she tells them.

I'm in the doorway, back behind the brass and percussion, nearly deafened sometimes by their sound. Yet the sound carries me. It helps that somewhere in the cello section, my son is part of all this. But I can't think past my joy. I can't put it into words.

∽

This particular symphony, Dvořák's ninth, old warhorse that it is, was a stunning accident in 1893, brand new and dumb luck, the result of unabashed enthusiasm one minute, a darker second-guessing the next. The Czech composer had been lured to New York for a couple of years to direct the National Conservatory of Music, an experiment established, in part, by the U.S. Congress, the first tuition-free music school open to all with talent, the first to recruit African Americans and women. Under Dvořák's influence, its democratic mission was never routine but charged with a deeper fever, *American* underscored. As a nationalist composer himself, mindful of Czech uneasiness in the all-encompassing Austrian Empire, he readily fell in with the school's founding principles though he seemed, at first, somewhat awed by the responsibility. "The Americans expect great things of me," he wrote home his second month here, "and the main thing is, so they say, to show them to the promised land of new and independent art, in short to create a national music. If the small Czech nation can have such musicians, they say, why could not they, too, when their country is so immense." The fact is that he, too, wanted young composers to take up fragments of song from *this* place, *this* time, though in this country—given our colonial past—the cultural influence to be thrown off was all of Europe, an idea that had seized American writers for some time, Whitman, for instance, calling many years earlier for literary rebellion, celebrating American life in his long, rambling lines, the frenzy and calm of that life, day and night, city and country. Though Dvořák's intent was for the moment pedagogical—"I came to America to discover what young Americans had in them, and to help them to express it"—he got immediately to work on his own version of what might reflect the American heart or at least his own energy translated by an American experience.

His symphony evolved quickly. Begun in January 1893, it was scored by the end of May, all except the trombone burst at the end, which Dvořák forgot to include until the first rehearsal some months later. It's often said that the raucous beginning echoes the chaotic streets and dockyards of New York. Or perhaps his fascination with trains started it, his listening at the railroad bridge over the Harlem

River or from the Bronx hillside he liked early in the day, a particularly fine place to gaze down at his favorite, the express to Chicago, its movement west embodying America to him, that cold-water leap into the new, the spirit dream most loved by Europeans who would never leave home, or would return, as he did, keeping faith with the old cities, the forests older than the cities or the ancient villages with names like Čermná and Zvěrkovice. Whether or not he had heard of Whitman's poem on the subject—"To a Locomotive in Winter"—I don't know, though it seems unlikely. But the two men were of one mind on the matter, both taken with this surreal and powerful bit of nineteenth-century technology. "Fierce-throated beauty," Whitman wrote almost twenty years earlier,

> Roll through my chant with all thy lawless music, thy
>   swinging lamps at night,
> Thy madly-whistled laughter, echoing, rumbling like an
>   earthquake, rousing all,
> Law of thyself complete, thine own track firmly holding, . . .
> Launch'd o'er the prairies wide, across the lakes,
> To the free skies unpent and glad and strong.

For Dvořák, watching the trains at the very start of such a journey those mornings in New York, it was all diesel smoke, great clouds of it rising as he listened, the massive wheels beginning to turn, their wheezing and clanging deranged as a bell made, then broken in anger on the forge, the arm raised then coming down until the pitch grew hard and steady as the train got smaller and gave itself to distance. One sound now unless you count the cello sobbing faintly underneath.

～

It's 2:45 at the Athenaeum, any Sunday afternoon, break time for the young musicians of the New World Orchestra. Nearly two hours of rehearsal so far, about an hour and a half to go. *I want those eighth notes absolutely staccato*, their director, Susan Kitterman, insists once, twice, three times over. It's been at least five runs through the passage in the last twenty minutes, gruelingly difficult because this is no dumbed-down version for kids. The orchestra plays—always—only the complete thing, exactly what each composer has scored. But now it's break, the instruments abruptly silenced in their cases or lowered carefully, cellos and string basses onto their sides to rest on the floor.

Musicians get hungry. At the back of the room is a cornucopia-in-waiting: cookies and carrot cake, vegetables and dip, chips of all persuasion, fruit drinks and soda provided by parents who have signed up for their turn months ago. There's a rush to the tables, paper plates piled high, drinks juggled. The kids wander off in small groups or in couples; individuals find a corner to themselves, pulling out a paperback, the plate balanced on their knees. Two violists, a clarinetist, someone on French horn remain behind for a few minutes, continuing work on a particularly hard measure until they too put down their instruments and head for the tables. The principal bassoonist is still discussing something with Kitterman, both poised intently over the score.

After a while, the co-principals of the cello section are back at their instruments, and it's a kind of quick, joyful pickup Vivaldi business that starts between them, just for the hell of it. In the corner, a few younger boys at their card game half laugh, half groan over a bad joke that's been making the rounds all afternoon. There are questions for Susan Bever, the orchestra manager, about the rehearsal schedule or a broken music stand or a slipping endpin. Many have ducked out for a moment—quick trips to the restrooms or outside where a small circle of the oldest kids talk softly over their glowing cigarettes. Back inside, near the drinking fountain, two girls show another a letter and watch expectantly as she reads. *Do you believe it?* says one, and they all roll their eyes to the ceiling. But by 3:10, nearly all are back in their seats running through their scales, checking their reeds, tightening their bows and drumheads, working their valves. Like great evil, whose mechanics are notoriously banal, this great good is profoundly matter-of-fact. These kids are serious musicians who love to play. And they play. The beauty they make—dark and shining—comes measure by measure. What's extraordinary is how ordinary it all seems.

~

It's probably impossible to figure when Dvořák's *New World Symphony* was first performed in Indianapolis, but it's surprising how early it could have been. Though records are spotty, depending on programs saved by concertgoers and given to various archives around the city, it's clear that all manner of musical groups were wildly active throughout the nineteenth century. One, in fact, played at the Athenaeum where the New World Youth Orchestra rehearses, an impressive solid wedding-cake of a building willed into life in the 1890s by the rebellious Turners, German immigrants whose culture was mind *and* body, a passionate mix of music, art, and athletics. Then called the Deutsche Haus—before the anti-German feeling of the First World War forced a name change—it hosted that early orchestra, the Musikverein, whose music from the period includes Dvořák's *Carnival*, an unruly overture with clashing brass and lovely string work. In 1911 the group changed its name to the Indianapolis Symphony, a move that may have increased its ambition because in 1916 its sixty members did perform, possibly premiering the *New World Symphony* in the city. On the religion page, below an article breathlessly headlined "New Serum to Bring Dead Back to Life," the reviewer at the *Indianapolis Star* was almost as enthusiastic about Dvořák's work, calling it "the most enjoyable feature of the afternoon," adding—how does one read this?—"but almost an hour was needed to play it."

Other orchestras may have attempted the symphony earlier. By 1895 Karl Schneider had founded his Indianapolis Philharmonic and certainly many visiting groups—the Cincinnati Orchestra, the Chicago Symphony, the Cleveland Orchestra—could have played the work. In 1921 Toscanini managed it, bringing his La Scala Orchestra from Milan for the occasion one Sunday afternoon in February. The city's major orchestra today—the Indianapolis Symphony Orchestra—came to life much later, in 1930, first playing at the Athenaeum, and though the initial seven years of programs are lost, it's certain that Dvořák's piece was performed in 1937 and often after that, a great favorite. By then the ISO was housed at the Murat Theatre, courtesy of the Shriners, whose outrageous taste in architecture was as far away from Dvořák's beloved Bohemia—or from Indiana—as could be thought or dreamt, their temple modeled after an Islamic mosque, tower and minaret rising up, the whole place cut with terra cotta trim, brown and yellow brick banding, windows of stained glass. Buried within was the Egyptian Room, its motifs drawn from the tombs of the upper Nile, a design planned well before Carter's 1922 discovery of King Tutankhamen's chambers, the image of that glamorous, spooky find raging through the popular imagination of the period. But longing makes for more longing. Perhaps the surreal displacement of Dvořák's music in such a place only deepened the Largo's "beautiful plaint of sorrow confided to the English horn," or so the program note for the earlier 1916 performance put it.

～

My first year out of college, I signed on as a full-time *searcher of lost books* at the University of Chicago's Regenstein Library—a more perfect job I'll never have, mythic and practical all at once. I remember my co-workers: Peter, a tall, quiet kid, a conscientious objector to the Vietnam War, inexplicably assigned to work out his alternative service as a clerk with us. Or mad Sharon, so intent on collecting fines, she'd drive at night on her own time to the addresses on the handwritten bookslips, armed with reading glasses and flashlight to figure out the illegible names and thus—at last, those bastards! she'd gleefully tell us—know whom to bill. *Searcher of lost deadbeats*, we called her.

But it's someone else who most comes back to me at odd moments, a fellow searcher slightly older than I was, who talked only of opera. The world stinks and people are rotten, he'd say, but I go home and put on records and hear truth in that singing—and passion, and real feeling. I loved his saying that, though he troubled me. I'd go home to my tiny one-room apartment and read and try to write until my friends came by, annoyed because—no phone and the foyer doorbell never worked—they had to shout up from the street to find me. But that opera guy—I thought him sad and melodramatic and sweet. He dreamed of going to live in Italy, Milan probably, where everyone, he said, was wild for opera, not like here. I used to stare at him when he wasn't looking, watch him as he stood shuffling through the small cards we searchers carried. It's just that he could so easily step from this world into another. For all that singing, there was a kind of silence around him as he worked at the monster card catalog or walked the stacks.

~

The year Dvořák arrived in New York—1892—was the year Whitman's life ended, at seventy-three, about a hundred miles south and west in Camden, New Jersey, but there are perhaps more intricate counterbalances. In the years following the height of Whitman's powers, when he was both ignored and occasionally lionized for *Leaves of Grass*—his eccentric, brilliant book, revised again and again from the mid-1860s well into the 1870s—Dvořák, quite a bit younger, was deepening his already impressive understanding of musical form. During that decade, he composed two symphonies, his first opera, a song cycle, all the while playing viola in the Czech National Orchestra, conducted those years by the great Smetana, whose greatness

Dvořák never doubted, though the friendship that would really change his life would begin a few years later when he met Brahms.

One can go back further. Dvořák was only six in 1847, already learning his father's multiple trades—butcher, innkeeper, village musician—and barely begun on the violin, getting his ears boxed for each wrong note, when Whitman underwent a conversion to music that would alter his own sense of how a poem could be made. By his own account, it was opera in particular that seized him. Perhaps its graceful, emphatic patchwork of sound moving through dramatic time drew him, but I suspect he loved how opera resists time too, aria as a way to stop and deepen it, then the recitative moving everything forward, caught against a pure orchestral sound that presses, releases, presses. "A new world," he wrote, "a liquid world—rushes like a torrent through you." Later he would claim outright the influences on his book: the Bible, Emerson, and opera, though this last, in its romantic frenzy, its violent shifts in tone—now tender or raucous, now tragic, now ecstatic—must have been the most immediate, spilling over into his sense of line and reach to make him question the old narrative way of longer poems. He worked fast and straight instead, without the slow-motion buffer of looking back, taking everything in present-tense flashes of image after image, casting them quiet, then into more expansive metaphor. "I hear the violoncello," he writes somewhere in the middle of "Song of Myself,"

> ('tis the young man's heart's complaint,)
> I hear the key'd cornet, it glides quickly in through my ears,
> It shakes mad-sweet pangs through my belly and breast.
>
> I hear the chorus, it is a grand opera,
> Ah this indeed is music—this suits me.
>
> A tenor large and fresh as the creation fills me,
> The orbic flex of his mouth is pouring and filling me full.

I hear the train'd soprano (what work with hers is this?)
The orchestra whirls me wider than Uranus flies,
It wrenches such ardors from me I did not know I possess'd
    them,
It sails me, I dab with bare feet, they are lick'd by the
    indolent waves,
I am cut by bitter and angry hail, I lose my breath,
Steep'd amid honey'd morphine, my windpipe throttled in
    fakes of death,
At length let up again to feel the puzzle of puzzles,
And that we call Being.

Later, in another section, "A Song of Occupations," the pace is calmer, the command more philosophical; its closure opens even as it understates itself. "All music is what awakens from you when you are reminded by the instruments," Whitman tells us,

It is not the violins and the cornets, it is not the oboe nor the
    beating drums, nor the score of the baritone singer sing-
    ing his sweet romanza, nor that of the men's chorus, nor
    that of the women's chorus,
It is nearer and farther than they.

I can't get over the notion that the instruments simply *remind* us of what's been there in the silence or in ourselves all along. Nearer *and* farther, Whitman insists. But music—from where exactly? There's no map for it.

∾

"We just came off this really sentimental violin line," Susan Kitterman is telling the clarinets at rehearsal, "and now *you're* the voice of rea-son." It's a playful, no-nonsense moment, just when everyone was dreaming off, caught in the flight of Dvořák's crescendo. Some of the kids nod, others lean forward and scribble something on their music, a few half smile at her remark. It's an astonishing thought to me, the notion that this music isn't just a wash of lovely, compelling sound but as complicated, as unpredictable as conversation, that one instrument answers another, one might even parody itself. Two might argue, one sober, one drunk; one is forgiving, one refuses; one knows only the simplest things, one loves the shadow world and won't give up its sad delirium, ever.

It slowly occurs to me that this isn't just some romantic reading foisted on a play of notes; I've actually begun to *hear* differently, not music at a distance but close up, how it's made, how it rises and falls, cuts itself off, stubbornly repeats, goes inward turning a minor key, bursting out again with a shift back to major into the bright world. And I wonder if what I'm beginning to hear in music is close to what I'm always wanting in poems, a way inward but at the same time, a way to love the world's complexity. Not to understand it really—is that ever possible?—but to co-exist with it.

Except to invite more of music's complication into poems—how exactly to do that? One varies syntax; one moves in and out of memory; one whispers or one's emphatic. *But what does it sound like?* I want to say about any poem I read now, any poem I try to write. Because that's where the secret reveals itself. It takes such patience, this spirit life; Dvořák's saying once that art is simply an elaboration on the smallest things we notice.

Yet what does it mean, in fact, to notice something? I think about Whitman noticing everything, his "Song of Myself" moving frame by frame, nearly cinematic, an unwieldy human kaleidoscope of detail about so many—the machinist, the senator, the farmer, the lunatic, the child being baptized, on and on. But Whitman's notice goes well beyond sight. "Now I will do nothing but listen," he writes,

> I hear bravuras of birds, bustle of growing wheat, gossip of
>   flames, clack of sticks cooking my meals.
> I hear the sound I love, the sound of the human voice,
> I hear all sounds running together, combined, fused or
>   following,
> Sounds of the city and sounds out of the city, sounds of the
>   day and night. . . .

So go the loping rangy lines Whitman invented by ear and eye, constructing this vast thing as if hoisting board upon board like the carpenter he was trained by his father to be. Everything, it seems, floods in. But the particular and memorable sound of the poem—that comes of his saying whatever he's saying again and again, bringing it up as if one long breath could really do it, aiming toward a form more musical than literary, the score's cherished repeats, the tenor ringing it out, the complexities of voice alone shading every human detail. Whitman worked from voluminous notes—hurried bits of comment, vignette, dream—hammering his prose down to its poetry, his ear to it, endlessly revising, second-guessing, exhausting himself. "To have a lovely thought is nothing remarkable," Dvořák told his students years later at the National Conservatory. "But to carry out a thought well and make something great of that . . . that is, in fact—art! How often a thing seems simple at first sight but in carrying it out such difficulties arise—I call them 'knots'—and you can't untie them, not if you were to do I don't know what."

Back in Indianapolis, Susan Kitterman is hard on the kids in this orchestra, exacting. "Bite the strings!" she calls out to the second violins. Then, waving everyone to stop, "You know what?" she says slowly. "I think you ought to practice this at home."

"A low blow," Susan Bever, the orchestra manager, whispers next to me.

But she begins again, working the passage over and over. "This is very, very tricky," she tells them. "You want that feeling of reaching farther than you really can."

~

All that American winter of 1893, while he worked on his symphony, Dvořák was obsessed with going home for the summer to his country place in Vysoká, far from Prague. Slowly though, as spring came with all green things stirring, he was caught by another idea. Inviting his whole family to join him in America, he would make the trip from New York to rural Spillville, Iowa, a Czech immigrant community, where, he was promised, his language was spoken right on the street. He had, just a couple of weeks earlier, put the finishing touches on his symphony "from the new world." Now he was speeding west through part of that world—Pennsylvania, then Ohio, then Indiana—on the very train he loved to watch from a distance in New York. There was a brief stop at Fort Wayne, Indiana. Maybe Dvořák stepped out onto the platform to buy sandwiches because someone decided everyone was hungry. About 140 miles south, in Indianapolis, no doubt there were kids just being kids who would grow up to become string, woodwind, and brass players, and, since the Indianapolis Symphony Orchestra at first recruited locally, it would be their fortunate lot to perform this piece so recently put to paper, the one still running through Dvořák's head, waking him up at night.

It's perhaps too tempting to go omniscient and follow this movie back quickly, like one of those time-lapse films that rush the seed into flower, then, in reverse, play its flourishing back to the merest speck. This isn't thought, of course. It's reverie. Back to 1893, and Dvořák continues on to Spillville and its facts, to a summer spent discovering the scarlet tanager, inviting its song into his music; or listening to his six children at play; or taking over the organ at St. Wenceslaus for early mass, working afternoons on an astonishing quartet, later dubbed his most "American" and thus its name. "Three months," he wrote home, "which will remain a happy memory for the rest of our lives." But part of this real dream is its specifically American darkness. "Few people and a great deal of empty space," he wrote back to a friend in Bohemia "And it is very 'wild' here and sometimes very sad—sad to despair. But habit is everything."

Meanwhile, I think past Dvořák's actual part in the movie to more imagined details: 1893, and of those kids in Indianapolis, say one will play—how many years from now?—the difficult English horn solo in the Largo that dips and turns and opens into the brain's most secret part, which remembers each distant particular and feels its chill. She's twelve; it's beginning to rain. From the porch, the windows wide open, she notices that back in the house her brother's voice is changing. It's funny, cracking on the word *crocus*. Or she hears how rain fills and overfills the wooden gutters, a pulse in that somehow, a low heartbeat. And what about this?—that downtown, three young violinists who will someday press and rage and release themselves to pure flight in Dvořák's third movement are now sitting cross-legged in the dirt at the edge of Michigan Street, under the rough lean-to that carpenters have slapped together, watching the new Deutsche Haus go up. One's bored out of his mind. But one kid's amused at how the canvas tarp billows out, the workmen shouting and whistling and reaching hard to pull it over the hoard of brick and lumber because of the rain, the wind so fierce, the scene blurring as if in Whitman's flashing present tense—Dvořák's Iowa to Indiana to right now, this moment. Why not? Everything's so all at once, finally. And is it music or poetry that such confusion isn't chaos?

In my old Catholic neighborhood in Chicago, we used to hear about the contemplatives, certain orders of nuns we never saw, cloistered away somewhere. The idea seemed scary and attractive and weird and what good did they do? Then we heard about the *holy rumble*, their job only to pray, words rushed like music, something near chant. One of our teachers told us—Sister Norbertus or Sister

Mary Hubertine?—that this sacred hum, exactly this, kept the earth turning on its axis, not merely this day or this minute but for all worlds of the past and the future because life is linked and there are no divisions in time. It's plain fact, she told us with nary a blink, like science is fact.

For proof, she instructed us to close our eyes and listen hard. She was right. We could hear it. The world *was* linked. That low-grade roar locked in our heads, steady undercurrent of rushing blood and flashing nerve—was it only that? Maybe it was those women after all, pulling from the world its oldest sound, every dark and light in the universe subdued, backdrop to thought, to words, to every sorrow coming up slowly, a forewarning or a reminder, the way Whitman's instruments remind. And I think about Dvořák, falling asleep those nights in Spillville, haunted by the symphony he's finished and set aside, its last ghost notes settling back to their first nothing. But it isn't nothing.

Sometimes I wander around the Athenaeum while the kids in the New World rehearse. I can sit easily enough in the back of the small auditorium where they play, dragging in a folding chair. Or I can join the handful of parents not from Indianapolis who, like me, come long distances to get here, waiting out the afternoon in the lobby on the plush benches that circle the pillars keeping the high ceiling at bay. Gone are the original Turners who came long ago from Germany, but down the hall are old photographs, little doors to elsewhere, turn-of-the-century water-stained shots of a singing class, of the lower school, of the kindergarten whose tiny charges have dropped their hands into a table of sand while their teacher stares blankly out into the future.

It's dark in that hallway, but I'm always surprised at the next photograph, how enormous and busy it is, blown-up and hand-colored to make an August night stay forever. *Ox-Barbecue*, the caption says,

1952, two years after I was born. Table after table set up in the Athenaeum's biergarten out back, the waiters in white jackets, it's way past dusk, little lights hanging from the trees, castor plants and four-o'clocks lining the dance floor, the band half blurring, instruments midair. These are the children and grandchildren of those who built this place and so many are dancing, so many still at the tables, leaning this way and that over their plates to catch something said under the music, the end of a joke, a crucial bit of story. I always figure that if I counted the dancers, then the vacant chairs, I'd come out even. But if I move abruptly, to the opposite wall, there's a more curious juxta-position—another photograph, same place, the biergarten blown-up huge and hand-colored again, this time with nothing in it at all, the band shell empty, the bare expanse of the dance floor suddenly so for-mal. Only the big-fisted castor plants remain, rows of four-o'clocks languid and zinnia straight up in the planters set along the walk. And I like to think that if I squinted hard at the crowded version, then turned quick and stared, I could call up those dancers, superimpose them, bring them back flushed and expectant out of that stilled August air.

~

Dvořák's visit to Iowa that summer, however brief, participated in a much larger dream of course, the nineteenth-century immigrant movement over the Atlantic to America and, for many, more westward still, into the heartland and beyond to yet another ocean. Certainly the Turners fleeing Germany in the 1840s, coming to unlikely places like Indianapolis, shared in this restlessness, a curiosity, really, of epic pro-portions that for good and ill captured much of the world's imagina-tion. Whitman, too, is said to have been changed by his own version of such a journey, taking his fourteen-year-old brother Jeff with him in 1848, west from Brooklyn and then south to spend three months working as a journalist for the *Crescent*, a recently established newspaper in New Orleans. But it wasn't so much that exotic, diverse city that altered Whitman's take on things; it was the work of getting there, about three weeks of hard travel by stage and riverboat, a trip that eventually, in the poet's view, assumed mythic scale as he got older, turning into months, even years of wandering in the retelling.

It was the vast loneliness of the country west that must have struck Whitman, the land's seeming endlessness, its desolation, which would gradually deepen and darken his vision, a crucial corrective for his jingoistic piety, his hail-fellow-well-met bluster. Taking the Ohio River, then turning south in Illinois to pick up the Mississippi, Whitman and his brother had little to do but watch mile after mile as bleak forest on both sides of the river unfolded, only occasional cabins and hardly a soul in sight. Paul Zweig, in his biography of Whitman, mentions a similar trip taken by Charles Dickens during an extended visit to America. His notes include a poignant scene no doubt enacted over and over since riverboats carried settlers as well as those, like Whitman, intent on less permanent adventures. "The men get out first," Dickens wrote of new homesteaders in Ohio,

> [they] help out the women; take out the bag, the chest, the chair; bid the rowers "goodby"; and shove the boat off for them. At the first plash of the oars in the water, the oldest woman of the party sits down in the old chair, close to the water's edge, without speaking a word. None of the others sit down, though the chest is large enough for many seats. They all stand where they landed as if stricken into stone; and look after the boat. . . . There they stand yet, without the motion of a hand. I can see them through my glass, when, in the distance and increasing darkness, they are mere specks to the eye.

One can imagine Whitman, too, quite lost in such a moment. "Few people and a great deal of empty space," Dvořák had written home from Iowa, "very sad, sad unto despair." And what depths open in us when we are so reminded?

Everything written about Dvořák's Ninth Symphony—his new world—eventually comes back to a kind of ache in the piece, coming up most profoundly in the Largo, its well-known second movement. And the origin of that sorrow? Some call up African American spirituals or Native American rhythms, both of which Dvořák praised and even suggested as heavily influencing the music before turning back on that notion to claim his homeland, its Bohemian melodies, as his spiritual source. And really, if we believe his letters or his friends' reminiscences, it was an abiding homesickness fueling this work written in New York that winter and spring of 1893, too far from his garden in Vysoká, his pigeons there, his favorite card game, *danka*, his walks with family and friends. Elements in folksong of whatever cultural stripe might call up the feel of a lost time and place. Surely the Largo in particular, its simple, plaintive lines of melody in spite of the elaborate orchestration, wakens melancholy in us. Maybe that's the poetry in Dvořák's method, his use of the folksong's pentatonic scale with its odd minor seventh, a half step up or down, a private hesitation where one might expect only the major's full step, its self-assured public sound; or the habit of returning over and over to a note, tonic or dominant, the sense of the elegiac in that lyric repetition, a looking back that weighs heavy.

"Goin' Home," of course, is the shorthand name of the Largo's memorable theme, an actual song culled from the symphony by William Arms Fisher, one of Dvořák's former students from the National Conservatory, after the composer's death in 1904. Immensely popular in the first third of this century, it was a staple in the piano repertoire of middle-class homes, though in my family, where irreverence was almost a hobby, the piece, at least in my mother's childhood, had a more practical use. So thoroughly recognized was "Goin' Home" by friends and acquaintances in the 1920s that if an afternoon visitor began to overstay her welcome, a sign from my grandmother—maybe her little finger touched her eyebrow—would send my mother to the piano to launch a small performance. "Some took the hint," my grandmother remarked dryly to me years later, "some didn't."

Not that this story ever altered the melody's power for her. Though it became a family tale I loved, I think in fact my grandmother told it as personal camouflage, a way to balance, even deny the embarrassingly deep effect the piece had on her. Those summers I stayed with her as a child, I listened as she played the song sometimes, late afternoon, though occasionally she'd stop, overcome for a moment before picking up the next measure, a slip neither she nor I ever spoke of. I wonder now what lost time or place the piece recalled for her, what moment she had buried that, because of some delicious, minor turn of sound, came up quick to stop her.

So music rewards us with its abundant sorrow, a curious form of happiness, or poetry does or any art that stills and darkens even as it gives us the shining world. That Dvořák's piece continues to move us is perhaps not a large miracle but a small one, this music so threatened by familiarity, an orchestral cliché by now, certainly one of the greatest hits, this crowd pleaser from its first performance in Carnegie Hall, where even that sophisticated audience willfully misbehaved, interrupting with wild applause after the second movement, shouting *Dvořák! Dvořák!* until he shyly rose from the back shadows of his box.

The symphony's continuing pull might be its peculiarly American feel, written as it was in the uneasy half-light between cultures. Dvořák as outsider, as immigrant—for the duration of its writing at least—plays out a universal American experience we'll probably never really shake, all those solitary elements in us that don't quite fit no matter how long our families have been here or what our circumstance. This is the desolate heart in Whitman's poems, too, for all their talkative energy bringing everything together. This double vision makes our connection to place, to most things probably, a spiritual act, which is to say, an act of will and imagination, not mere accident of biology or history. It's true that the Athenaeum, its biergarten and rathskeller so lovingly reproduced, went up as a kind of wish to bring the old world here, a Bavarian castle grafted solidly on new world swamp and prairie. And for that, its longing is the longing of Dvořák's Largo, a homesickness. But that dramatic juxtaposition moves the imagination forward as well as back, an heroic nerve in that, as if one could really live there, in the future, with everything one's lived brought vividly along, as if there was a plan howbeit close to dream.

~

It's the hour's drive home to West Lafayette that I dread, especially after the occasional late rehearsals that stretch into evening. Everyone is tired. Going over Dvořák's lively scherzo, Susan Kitterman calls out, "I don't want it beautiful, I want it feverish," and there's one last fierce upping of energy in the room. "Good," she says, "good. We're doing wonderfully." Now the kids are packing up, putting away their music stands. Some still joke and talk, the brass players especially refusing to give up, giddy with exhaustion, launching impromptu into *Ain't Misbehavin'*. "Go home already!" a violinist yells over to them, laughing. My son is worn out, I can tell; the cello case takes both arms now. It seems enormous, bigger than before; he's listing to one side as he steers it through the crowd of parents come to pick up their kids.

I may dread the drive, but I look forward to my son's stories of who said what outrageous thing or his delight at certain parts of the music—did you hear that neat place in the Dvořák, he asks, where it's just a string quartet playing? He's flipping the dial on our radio until something stops him. We argue about it—is it Mozart or Haydn? I'm sure it's Mozart, he says.

It's late but because of that it's cooler now, and we decide to take back roads, not I-65 but 421, then over on 28. We'll avoid the construction that way, and driving a little slower, we can open the windows, the fields giving off their sweetness—something's just been cut. One of Beethoven's late quartets comes on, one he wrote after he'd gone totally deaf. I turn to tell my son this but he's fallen asleep. It's dark by now, the fields black but wild with fireflies doing their slow blink off and on.

There's a bit near the end of Dvořák's Largo, maybe my favorite part, where everything drops down to nothing for a few measures, not even one violin or a small whistling of flute keeps the momentum. It's startling, this happening once. But it happens again not much later, and then a third time, long enough that each pause deepens to a genuine absence—eerie, this widening hole in the music. I never know quite what to make of it or of the pleasure it brings. Everything held back suddenly, the world beyond—a rich, grave silence—offering itself like that.

Bishop's Blue Pharmacy

A year before her death, Elizabeth Bishop finished a poem, "Santa-rém," which placed her in the crux of the marvelous, at the conflux of two of the world's great rivers, the Amazon and the Tapajós. The poem rings with exotic, chaotic life—carts hooked up to zebus, those curly-horned oxen; young nuns waving, still in their blinding white habits, off to a downriver mission by steamer; the whole lovely racket of departure and arrival. But this is mere overture; the revelation lies in wait, and the poem gradually narrows to its delivery. Entering a "blue pharmacy," as she calls it, the poet discovers a wasps' nest, empty, and placed lovingly on a shelf. "Small, exquisite," she tells us, "clean matte white, / and hard as stucco." Eventually, perhaps amused by her interest, the pharmacist gives it to her, and she carries off her prize to the waiting ship. There, a Mr. Swan, fellow passenger and retiring head of Philips Electric—"really a very nice old man," Bishop assures us—blurts out simply, "What's that ugly thing?" And so, on such a question, the poem ends.

I can run this through my head a thousand times and I still return to that moment amid the dusty bottles and boxes, what I imagine to be the peculiar shade of that "blue pharmacy." It's the surprise of that gleaming, tidy relic—the wasps' nest high in its honored place—that stops me, how a simple image presses into memory as fuse and heart to make a poem, to demand that it unfold, that it keep unfolding.

Surprise. How that is linked to finding, to finding *out.* I think of once finding something similar, a map but a wholly different kind of map, a quick, aerial retake on the earth calling itself "The Top of the World," its center not Asia or America or Europe but the north pole and its arctic air, frozen islands by the hundreds, strips of cold blue— a map, in short, governed by nothing *but* surprise, that love of the odd angle. There it was at a garage sale a few summers ago, leaning against the paint-dripped bookcase, next to the wingback chair. I stood and stared. This may be one of those indulgent, dream-lit moments, but I am thinking Elizabeth Bishop would have been equally smitten, not as much as with the wasps' nest probably, but enough to have outbid me for it at the edge of that slow backyard, overgrown with anthemis and delphinium and poppy.

The yard itself—about a fourth acre packed with the tall, rangy flowers, blue, blood-red—was eye-level, an ocean. Bishop would have liked that too, how it made a person tiny and awestruck like those Chinese paintings, all mountain and gorge, the little bit of a man visible in the lower left corner, looking up. I may be digressing, but digression is how Bishop builds her vision: an image, then scene after scene until we know the whole moving direction of the mind. Enclose the full morning, then—the crumbling driveway up to the old house, the cellar odds and ends on the grass and the steps, the map, this "Top of the World" lifted up for inspection, and beyond, that blaze of color, blue and red, untended, gone to a defiant beauty. Enclose it and we'd have something close to a poem, for no doubt the urgent delphinium, the languid poppy, would launch us in their cross angles right out of that careful, false enclosure—the poem—and into a secret sense of things, however cluttered or dangerous. Poems do that; they take us somewhere else even as their words dissolve and we're back into the common world now too rich, almost, to figure. Bishop's poems do this thing, *transport*, and they do it with uncommon grace and life.

Her own life, of course, was vivid with movement. Born in 1911 in

Massachusetts and raised by her grandparents there and in Nova Scotia, Bishop lived in New York and in Europe, in Key West and in Mexico, until, on a fluke when she was forty, she traveled to South America by tramp steamer, stopping in Brazil for a three-day visit. How three days stretched into eighteen years is a matter far beyond mathematics. Her friend and partner there, Lota de Macedo Soares, with whom she lived those years, brought her immediately into the Brazilian artistic and intellectual community. "I don't feel 'out of touch' or 'expatriated' or anything like that," she wrote Robert Lowell some months after she had settled. "I was always too shy to have much 'intercommunication' in New York anyway, and I was miserably lonely there most of the time—here I am extremely happy, for the first time in my life." She got there in 1951, writing "Arrival at Santos" in the weeks that followed. In that poem's fresh inventory, the way its humor flashes to combine the domestic and the strange, we have that curious energy that is pure Bishop.

"Here is a coast; here is a harbor," she begins with a child's accuracy.

> here, after a meager diet of horizon, is some scenery:
> impractically shaped and—who knows?—self-pitying
>   mountains,
> sad and harsh beneath their frivolous greenery,
>
> with a little church on top of one. And warehouses,
> some of them painted a feeble pink, or blue,
> and some tall, uncertain palms. Oh, tourist,
> is this how this country is going to answer you
>
> and your immodest demands for a different world,
> and a better life, and complete comprehension
> of both at last, and immediately,
> after eighteen days of suspension?

What begins as a simple listing quickly deepens into the adult's real view cut with irony and common sense, the joke not on the country but on the short-sighted tourist or the self-effacing speaker herself. Bishop is tough, impatient with what is falsely romantic, what memory would mindlessly prize, so cool and unblemished. The *picturesque*—it just won't go, not with these "self-pitying mountains" or the "tall, uncertain palms."

"Finish your breakfast," she goes on in her no-nonsense way.

> . . . The tender is coming,
> a strange and ancient craft, flying a strange and brilliant rag.
> So that's the flag. I never saw it before.
> I somehow never thought of there *being* a flag,
>
> but of course there was, all along. And coins, I presume,
> and paper money; they remain to be seen.
> And gingerly now we climb down the ladder backward,
> myself and a fellow passenger named Miss Breen,
>
> descending into the midst of twenty-six freighters
> waiting to be loaded with green coffee beans.
> Please, boy, do be more careful with that boat hook!
> Watch out! Oh! It has caught Miss Breen's
>
> skirt! There! Miss Breen is about seventy,
> a retired police lieutenant, six feet tall,
> with beautiful bright blue eyes and a kind expression.
> Her home, when she is at home, is in Glens Fall
>
> s, New York. . . .

Miss Breen—what luck to find her!—is the poem's three-dimensional gift, a kind of holograph of sturdy goodwill standing in relief before the sad mountains and warehouses encircled by the busy harbor. Against the horizontal, that distant first layering of landscape, Bishop sets this very vertical police lieutenant in her gravely comic descent into the waiting boat, not a digression at all but the thickening, *knowable* thread in this foreign weave that threatens so easily to slip out of reach, already out of expectation. Glens Falls, New York, check; six feet tall, check; retired, seventy years old, check; beautiful bright blue eyes, yes. These prosaic details return us to ourselves and the wonder—so much in Bishop's work—of how the trivial sustains us. "There," Bishop continues. "We are settled." And in that understated line, one feels a universe rising and falling.

> The customs officials will speak English, we hope,
> and leave us our bourbon and cigarettes.
> Ports are necessities, like postage stamps, or soap,
>
> but they seldom seem to care what impression they make,
> or, like this, only attempt, since it does not matter,
> the unassertive colors of soap, or postage stamps—
> wasting away like the former, slipping the way the latter
>
> do when we mail the letters we wrote on the boat,
> either because the glue here is very inferior
> or because of the heat.

If we pause here, we might be breathless after this rush of surface fact and interpretation. And in this silence, the poem's revelation is abruptly pitched. "We leave Santos at once," Bishop tells us, "we are driving to the interior."

That interior—the central mystery in Bishop's work—is the destination she most maps us toward, however offhand her way might be. In a much later poem, "The Moose," finished in 1972, Bishop carefully evokes the close magic of an overnight bus ride, the coastal road running like some marvelous ribbon down from Canada to

Boston. The point, of course, is the moose itself; it makes its godlike entrance from the midnight woods and stops the bus cold—"towering, antlerless," the poet says, seeming "high as a church / homely as a house" to the amazed, nearly speechless passengers. But the moments that earn this spectacle come earlier in a more familiar, cozier dark. Here, amid the others' snores and long sighs, we almost lose the speaker to what she calls her "dreamy divagation," her "gentle, auditory, / slow hallucination," which brings up from the back of the bus "Grandparents' voices"

> uninterruptedly
> talking, in Eternity:
> names being mentioned,
> things cleared up finally;
> what he said, what she said,
> who got pensioned;
>
> deaths, deaths and sicknesses;
> the year he remarried;
> the year (something) happened.
> She died in childbirth.
> That was the son lost
> when the schooner foundered.
>
> He took to drink. Yes.
> She went to the bad.
> When Amos began to pray
> even in the store and
> finally the family had
> to put him away.
>
> "Yes . . ." that peculiar
> affirmative. "Yes . . ."

A sharp, indrawn breath,
half groan, half acceptance,
that means "Life's like that.
We know *it* (also death)."

Talking the way they talked
in the old featherbed
peacefully, on and on,
dim lamplight in the hall,
down in the kitchen, the dog
tucked in her shawl.

From this dense resource of memory—the *half*-remembered—
we are wrenched into what seems, though it is not, the grandest hallucination of all, the ghostly moose out on the macadam. This is
Bishop's dramatic sense at work, how she moves the mind quickly or
languidly, layering scene and gesture as backdrop like some richly
tinted geological map we cut through to reach the earth's iridescent
core. But her touch is so light that we are never cornered into insight
or burdened by its presence. From this comes the quiet moral radiance of her poems, a tone neither insistent nor bombastic but nevertheless brimming with the capacity to see and feel. There is no pretense here, no self-important reach for the higher ground. "I feel my
way through a poem," she has said. "[A] phrase may find its way into
my head like something floating in the sea, and presently, it attracts
others to it." So this creature, the poem, begins to happen the way
meaning really happens, not with quick, forgettable hype but memorably, over time. Even the love poem, a form usually caught up in
some sort of amplification or urgency, tends to loosen and widen in
her hands. Poems such as "The Shampoo" or her famous villanelle,
"One Art," keep to a movement and a tone largely happenstance, this
in spite of the press of their traditional cadence and rhyme. One

thinks of Bishop's friend, Marianne Moore, and her remark that "the deepest feeling always shows itself . . . / not in silence, but restraint." Just so, it is Bishop's restraint that suggests the passion behind it, things *almost* past control.

However effortlessly her poems give way, her manner of working was a conscious choice made early in life when she discovered the work of George Herbert and Gerard Manley Hopkins, poets whose style she called "baroque," something close to what she wanted in her own work: "To portray," as she was to quote M. W. Croll for a college paper, "not a thought, but the mind thinking," that moment "in which the truth is still *imagined*." Writing not merely to copy experience but in fact to *have* it, to catch thought in all its wayward flashing turns, invites that crucial element in good poetry, that surprise so valued by Bishop. Her affection for William Carlos Williams's poem "The Sea-Elephant," for example, lay in how she saw his swift transition, something hushed then exclaimed, this wonder turned bravado.

> Trundled from
> the strangeness of the sea—
> a kind of
> heaven—
>
> Ladies and Gentleman!
> . . . the gigantic
> sea-elephant! O wallow
> of flesh . . .

In the class she taught at Harvard (this noted by one of her students there, Dana Gioia), she praised the poem for such leaps, though for her its finest moment was the nerve of its "Blouaugh," a word coined by Williams for the elephant's roar coming next. It's easy to see why Bishop loved the present tense, given the immediate circuitry in much of her work, though often she switches tense, as she once claimed in interview, for "depth, space, foreground, background." This is how the mind works, after all; we think about yesterday, say, then this minute's push and pull, then some brightly imagined Sunday afternoon three weeks from now. So the poem *right here* finds perspective, context, place.

Such layering lends dramatic force to Bishop's weave of image and scene. In an earlier poem, "Over 2,000 Illustrations and a Complete Concordance," the poet begins in the present, this moment, bent over an enormous Bible and its slow, elegant drawings. "Thus should have been our travels," she decides, "serious, engravable." Then with typical precision, she follows "the Tomb, the Pit, the Sepulcher," the date-palm branches that "look like files," the "birds / suspended on invisible threads above the Site"—scenes struck for something, clearly, some classic meaning.

Not so the speaker's own travels that are taken up next, one by one in honest recollection. Here mainly is loud, unblinking incongruity, hardly engravable: a dead man, in Mexico, for instance, decked out in a "blue arcade" against the blaring jukebox and its "Ay, Jalisco!" or at Marrakesh, the "pockmarked prostitutes / . . . their tea-trays on their heads / . . . naked and giggling / . . . asking for cigarettes." But it wasn't those sad women who seemed most frightening; it was the "holy grave," the poet tells us, "not looking particularly holy / . . . open to every wind from the pink desert / . . . half-filled with dust, not even the dust / of the poor prophet . . . who once lay there." Her Arab guide stands looking on, amused at such distress—or such innocence.

Travels: serious, yes, but engravable? "Everything only connected by 'and' and 'and,'" Bishop writes. For how, really, to arrange such troubling scenes for meaning, how to add connectives that guide and give perspective, not the neutral *and* but the more precise teachers, the *because* and the *though* or the quick and hopeful *if*. "Open the book," the poet says at last.

Open the heavy book. Why couldn't we have seen
this old Nativity while we were at it?
—the dark ajar, the rocks breaking with light,
an undisturbed, unbreathing flame,
colorless, sparkless, freely fed on straw,
and, lulled within, a family with pets,
—and looked and looked our infant sight away.

This ending irony, where only *imagined* truth has any beauty, is a
fine catch in the throat. Yet the specifics of such invention stubbornly
carry their own vitality, regardless of the poem's dark intentions. No
matter how carefully Bishop chooses detail to deepen and buoy up
that spirit of ennui, her own "infant sight" surfaces anyway in her
unmistakable slant on things that cuts through years of culture's
droning overlay to see things new. Imagine anyone but Bishop calling
the age-old crèche pose—the Virgin and her child, and Joseph and
how many warm-breathed beasts—simply "a family with pets." Such
small turns are vivid points of color and life; she sees bread made with
cornmeal in a Rio bakery as "yellow-fever victims / laid out in a
crowded ward," a boarded-up beach house as "a sort of artichoke of
a house, but greener," a young cousin's coffin as "a little frosted cake."
It is often her humor, coming into the gravest of subjects, that both
unnerves and disarms us.

This humor, evident in so many of her poems, is for me of the
most cherished sort: affectionately ironic toward convention, quirky,
sprung from an odd though immensely sane intelligence. For Bishop,
it was a matter of art *and* life. One story might be characteristic, one
she told Randall Jarrell about her ride with Marianne Moore to the
burial in 1949 of Moore's mother, with whom Moore lived for over
half a century. The car was thick with a mournful silence until Bishop,
who had for years shared the older poet's love of the exotic—
circuses, zoos, amusement parks—noticed a small sign along the

road. "See the Little Reptile Farm," she read out loud. Moore, she told Jarrell, looked up hopefully; then, remembering where she was, and why, dropped once more into her sorrow. Count one second. Two. Then—"Maybe on the way back," she whispered to Bishop.

That Bishop herself loved this story makes clearer for me what I find so striking in her work, the way her poems resist what is predictable, the polite *should* of their circumstance, and find instead their own shape and revelation. Just as Bishop, given the conventions of grief, *should* have stifled her wish to read that sign aloud, so *should* the narrator, Robinson Crusoe in her poem "Crusoe in England," feel well rid of his godforsaken island and glad to be back in London. He is—but the whole truth? It is those makeshift relics—his flute, his parasol, his shriveled shoes—that will not release.

> The knife there on the shelf—
> it reeked of meaning, like a crucifix.
> It lived. How many years did I
> beg it, implore it, not to break?
> I knew each nick and scratch by heart,
> the bluish blade, the broken tip. . . .
> Now it won't look at me at all.

So often Bishop's stance invites these turns; it is easy to be overcome by their lived, homemade, even ridiculous beauty. For all the alleged personal reserve of her poems and her own impatience with the so-called confessional poets—"they seldom have anything interesting to confess anyway," she once said in interview, "or a lot of things I should think were best unsaid"—the power of her images, Crusoe's heartbreaking objects among them, is in how they reveal the human interior, those elements in ourselves cherished precisely because they are not public, though their deep chemistry can both delight and defeat. "As a child," Bishop wrote, "I used to look at my grandfather's

Bible under a powerful reading-glass. The letters . . . were suddenly as big as life, as alive, and rainbow-edged. It seemed to illuminate as it magnified; it could also be used as a burning glass."

Her poem "In the Waiting Room," from her last collection, *Geography III*, makes us conscious of this dangerous double wealth, illumination and its fire. Immediately we are pressed back to 1918, to Worcester, Massachusetts, where the poet recalls exactly how it was to wait for her silly Aunt Consuelo in the dentist's outer office, riveted to the lurid *National Geographic*, its black volcano "spilling . . . rivulets of fire" as remote and alarming as the image on another page, that "dead man slung on a pole / —'Long Pig,' the caption said." On and on, the child keeps reading—"I was too shy to stop," she tells us—until from the inside office, this "*oh!* of pain / —Aunt Consuelo's voice." But for Bishop, who's so careful to invoke the lamplit, overheated room, the piles of overcoats, the rising feverish pitch of those *National Geographic* pages ("Their breasts were horrifying"), a greater shock is coming.

> . . . it was *me:*
> my voice, in my mouth.
> Without thinking at all
> I was my foolish aunt,
> I—we—were falling, falling,
> our eyes glued to the cover
> of the *National Geographic*,
> February, 1918.

What follows is the frantic, puzzled disorder of thought itself—questions, reassurances ("I said to myself: three days / and you'll be seven years old") about who is who, where lines fall between the self and the world. For anyone but Bishop, this might have become a dreadful, heavy-handed passage, full of abstract melodrama. Here it flies, panic complete with the child's disembodied view.

I gave a sidelong glance
—I couldn't see any higher—
at shadowy gray knees,
trousers and skirts and boots
and different pairs of hands
lying under the lamps.
I knew that nothing stranger
had ever happened. . . .
Why should I be my aunt,
or me, or anyone?

Bishop gives us more of this, and more—"a big black wave, /
another, and another"—until she pulls us out by telling us simply,

The War was on. Outside,
in Worcester, Massachusetts,
were night and slush and cold,
and it was still the fifth
of February, 1918.

That the discovery of self is pinned to a simultaneous discovery of
the attendant world is, perhaps, an old idea, but newly alive in this
poem. In taking up carefully what we see, that which pleases us or
darkly stuns, we define ourselves anyway. The important thing, she
wrote once to Anne Stevenson, lay elsewhere, in something absolutely crucial for art and its creation: "a self-forgetful, perfectly useless
concentration."

Useless? As useless, perhaps, as her wry, luminous wasps' nest,
high as treasure in that remote blue pharmacy. Or as useless, I suppose, as the wonder that fills us sometimes, before we even think
about it, with a rare, self-forgetful joy.

POETRY'S OVER AND OVER

Maybe it was 1973. I know it was Hyde Park, our friend John sitting with a group of us on break in the University of Chicago's Regenstein Library where I worked as a searcher of lost books. This was the vending room, full of buzzing Coke and candy-bar machines. Impossible years now, all of us in our twenties, and John—how to say it?—caught up in an anguish of the dearest sort, trying to tell us, yes, he had seen her upstairs in the reading room, this someone he'd noticed for months. He had just spotted her *moments ago*, and finally he had spoken. So what did she say? we asked, fearing the worst. After all, she was smart and spritelike and gorgeous. And John? Well, John was like us. She said "hi," he said with a kind of odd, lit-up hesitation. Then, rousing: only it wasn't, you know, "hi"—it was *hi*. Sort of like this—*hi*. And he tried to look like her or the way he imagined she looked: cheered by his attention, intrigued. Not "hi," he said again, but *hi*. And he looked at us expectantly, repeating that young woman's simple greeting maybe six or seven times, each more weighted for him than the last—her *hi* not "hi" at all but *hi*, a world within that, powerful enough to open some vast future.

We nodded, though, to be honest, each *hi* sounded pretty much the same to me, on the scale of one to ten in the great order of *hi-dom*, about average, a four or a five. Still, we nodded. Of course we nodded. John was our friend; we wished him the best. What does it take to break a heart, then or now? The tables were formica, the astroturf on the floor stained with god knows what. But there was John almost triumphant, caught up in his guesswork, no, *certain*, past guesswork via that one word, over and over, the curious mantra of it, a piece of rope held out over the abyss. Poor rope! But there's power in that, no matter how small the thing repeated. Even now, maybe especially now nearly thirty years later, my husband and I can call up this moment— and do—as metaphor, as template, a thing some hopeless new experience might remind us of and echo. We only have to say to each other—in the way of the long married—"she said *hi*" and John's face, its gentle urgency, comes back. And the rest of us come back too, eyeing each other around that table, not, for once, laughing, touched by such delicate and really pointless longing.

I admit I love this story, and feel lucky to have witnessed it. John's desperate wish to make meaning where there was none is, I suppose, the moving thing, but his passionate repeated examination of that most conventional utterance reaches back somewhere—to childhood lullabies that scare the dark, to ancient rituals that draw in the beast without violence, to some point where fate is clear, exact, and— surprisingly—what is wanted after all. Maybe it's not as hard as I thought to define poetry.

～

More and more, it's the obvious that turns mysterious on us. For instance, that this thing, poetry, that Wallace Stevens claimed existed in the world whether poems were written or not, has something profoundly to do with how things repeat, that things repeat at all, why they can't help repeating. I mean this, for starters, in the most clichéd and unconscious physical way—heart and lungs with their endless in and out; inevitable fall, past the cold dark, year after year to inevitable spring; cells repeated uncountably so the child grows up, grows *other*, into not-just-a-child; the way the body itself, so my friend Pat DeFlaun in nursing school tells me, is so wedded to the good repeat

that any departure—one heartbeat skipped, one cell going haywire—
is suspect and possibly pathological. So the body's arsenal rushes to
fix things, white cells flashing, pacemaker renotching the faulty
rhythm to regain the plain old, plain old. And we wait for that familiar cadence in spite of our contemporary hunger for invention and
pledge of allegiance to Ezra Pound's great call to poets to "make it
new." It's exactly the way I wait these mornings I write, my teenage
son downstairs slowly riding the anguished notes upward, practicing
again and again past his doubts and swearing stops/starts the first
movement of Elgar's cello concerto, its own darkened *if only, if only*,
and my relishing it more, each time.

In musicology, the whole notion of repetition, redundancy, the
repeat has been studied way past anyone's patience, of course, the
why of its effect to a large extent as physiological and primal as anything governed by heart or lungs. It might be a matter of simple fuel,
the resources needed to stay with a run of music (or, for that matter, a
run of words). One is alert, pressed forward, a receiver; a kind of tension is set into place. Then something *comes back*, something heard or
seen before. What happens in such a moment? In poetry, the critic
Harvey Gross has suggested that any repeated business is a "voiced
pause," a trick in a way, a method of claiming silence while not being
silent at all. In music, there's a similar read on this; but more, repetition is less static, thought to concern the "economics of dynamic psychology," or so Heinz Kohut and Siegmund Levarie called it in an
article first published fifty years ago. The *economics* of the thing. So
it's an exchange, a fluid arrangement. But they go further, into a more
astonishing discovery. It's just that "when hearing a phrase or a
melody for the second time," these two, a doctor and a psychologist,
wrote, "the listener saves a part of the energy required for a first hearing. He recognizes it, that is, [it] requires less effort to master it than
when it was new. The surplus energy is one of the sources which
enable the listener to experience joy."

I have to say this floored me. All the extra energy saved by the repeat—the body actually *reads* that as joy. So that's what happens every time I listen to Samuel Barber's Violin Concerto, the poignant solo once established by violin, taken up how many times by flute and other instruments in the orchestra, though my sense of what is called "joy" in this context contains all manner of other riches that comfort and sustain—sadness, for one, regret or the faintest of hope. The point is one literally feels it; according to researchers, it's *physical*, this powerful response because energy—one might even say calories—are actually saved back and released as small explosions within. In a way, one just lets go. One doesn't have to *do* or understand. The sound glides over and under and wherever sound goes. One deepens and dreams exactly because one doesn't rush forward, all ears and tension. It's suddenly obvious why Freud might want to connect repetition with that final peacemaker, the death instinct. Or why the word "repeat"—according to my linguist friend Mary Niepokuj—shares an ancient Indo-European root with the word "feather." One's released, in flight, somehow suspended into a small nowhere for a moment. If art *is* a drug, this is surely one sweet reason for addiction.

That small nowhere in a poem such as Philip Larkin's "Toads Revisited" gradually exudes a similar solacing melancholy and largely through its repetition, this meditation of a working person on the plight of the old who no longer work, who can now glory in walks in the park and watching people, who have no hours to keep. All these *shoulds* of retirement, which, in an entirely perverse Larkinesque way, get turned upside down: it simply isn't like that, not at all, or so suggests our dry-eyed realist speaker. Of those one might "meet of an afternoon,"

> Palsied old step-takers
> Hare-eyed clerks with the jitters,

Waxed-fleshed out-patients
Still vague from accidents,
And characters in long coats
Deep in the litter-baskets—

All dodging the toad work
By being stupid or weak.
Think of being them!
Hearing the hours chime,

Watching the bread delivered,
The sun by clouds covered,
The children going home;
Think of being them,

Turning over their failures
By some bed of lobelias. . . .

There's a comparison coming next, the speaker of the poem putting all this against his own tedious workaday lot of in-trays and the
"shall-I-keep-the-call-in-Sir" and coming out—barely—the winner.
It might be the closest we get to an admission of personal happiness
in Larkin. But we linger in this passage about the old men, the poet
taking time with his images, giving them teeth and substance. More,
it's the use of that one line that sharpens and throws everything into
relief—*Think of being them!*—first as exclamation, astonishment
registered, and later, more internalized and grave, cast as declaration, nearly whispered, an idea connected to the thought of failure,
the thought of turning that failure over and over. The fact that
Larkin sets the lines as direct address works the public, rhetorical
pulse that runs this poem from the start even as it reaches beneath
that to a thing more private and disturbing, particularly in the second instance. "Think of being them," he no longer announces but

offers more quietly, now a fact told to the self to be worried through, absorbed. It's probably no accident that the repetition carries this deeply interior feel—we're in that suspended state of "the voiced pause" after all—and there's energy released because all forward narrative motion is stalled for a moment. We don't need to be racing anywhere.

There's something even more unnerving going on. Elsewhere in the research that musicologists do, one finds repetition often connected to danger, to fate, especially if the repeated tones are short, spaced evenly and followed by a longer, more emphatic note. An often used example: the famous unto cliché opening of Beethoven's Fifth Symphony, the old *da-da-da-daaa* that foretells such doom. Larkin's repeated *think of being them* with its deliberate single stresses sets up a personal threat that will gradually take over the poem. "Nowhere to go but indoors," he continues in that final section,

> No friends but empty chairs—
>
> No, give me my in-tray,
> My loaf-haired secretary,
> My shall-I-keep-the-call-in-Sir:
> What else can I answer,
>
> When the lights come on at four
> At the end of another year?
> Give me your arm, old toad;
> Help me down the Cemetery Road.

By the end, in spite of that brave hail-fellow-well-met flourish of "no, give me my in-tray," the earlier identification is sinking in. "Give me your arm, old toad; / Help me down the Cemetery Road," Larkin writes in the evenly balanced final two lines, the poem closing out in the far more conventional presence of end-rhymes—yet another kind of repeating—the lost, nearly archaic sound of the couplet now, its pure unyielding ballast.

～

Repetition in this double mode, as release and anchor, exhilaration and threat, is nowhere more evident than in the various forms devised for poems over time. It has been said by critic Paul Fussell that the study of poetry is the study of pattern, which, he says, is the study of repetition. And certainly all our standard poetic shapes, first devised for music or to learn by heart for recitation, repeat themselves emphatically for both the pleasure of the sound and to underscore meaning. The villanelle, for instance, developed in France from an older Italian folk song/dance structure somewhere in the sixteenth century, still carries its original lively, almost whimsical impulse, although its full-line repetitions—Elizabeth Bishop's "the art of losing isn't hard to master" from her well-known poem "One Art," for instance—have grown darker in the last century, the playfulness gradually more ironic, the repeats more disturbing. In Bishop's case, the main recurring line is pretty *un*identical by the final stanza—"it's evident / the art of losing's not too hard to master," things going haywire now with the added words "not" and "too," as if there's order in the world all right but its fate is to be disrupted. In the psychology of music, it's understood that any blockage, any change in expectation—in tempo, key, dynamics—creates an emotional response in the listener; one is moved or exalted or saddened. So comes genuine power in poetry too, from some small misstep, some slightly skewed image or cadence—the *just when* we assume something will happen. And guess what? It doesn't, or it does—but not exactly as we thought. No, Bishop tells us, her cheerful credibility slipping now, "the art of losing's not *too* hard to master." We feel that darkened shift a way into grief; this small variation hits hard, bringing us into the real subject of the poem. Even Fussell cites such "imbalance" as the crucial thing of poetry, quoting Swinburne to back him up: "There can be no verse where there is no modulation."

But modulation only works when the bass line is clear, and bass line repetition floods our traditional forms. The sestina, an incredibly complicated creature invented by what must have been some very bored troubadours, uses repeated words throughout—at the end of lines, and cast more thickly in the final stanza—to make a dense, seemingly obsessive richness. Or the ballad, with its famous refrain taking us back to the real point of things—how many times? Then, of course, we have the sonnet, said most to resemble the way humans actually think; that is, problem set up and—bingo!—solved or at least argued to death, the rhyme throughout simply repeated pressure points on whatever matter *is* the matter, the answer set with simplicity and often majesty by the ending couplet. All these forms show us again that poetry is fashioned, *put together*, that art is, in part at least, artifice, that the oldest root of our word *"make"* is *mag*, "to knead," be it clay for bricks or dough for bread, yet another repetitive motion at the heart of human survival.

One of our most venerable shapes, the litany, is something that has haunted us from the start, back there amid all that busy "magging," especially in its connection to religious incantatory traditions; the Bible, of course, is part of this but also the Bhagavad-Gita and the Koran. This is repetition writ large, frozen into forms that seem powered by forces beyond the self, more a communal sound, not, on the face of it, anything as quirky as Larkin's recurring line in "Toads Revisited." Sometimes though, in contemporary use, the old and new mix in surprising ways as in—to bring up music again—Cole Porter's "Night and Day" where at the very start one note repeats thirty-five times, an idea inspired by the composer's travels in the Middle East. It was the muezzin he couldn't shake, his lovely, lonely summoning of worshippers to prayer.

To break down the litany is to break down the treasure to its smallest crucial part. There's the anaphora, a thing from the Greeks meaning "a carrying up or back." In fact, this repeated word or phrase does release new moves, *carrying up* as the poem progresses, and, by way of its seemingly static position in the line, *carrying back* as well, a double, contradictory effort that keeps a powerful pulse going. Walt Whitman comes to mind instantly, Whitman everywhere really, the following dark, almost manic rendering of serious illness in the "To Think of Time" section of *Leaves of Grass* just an example:

> When the dull nights are over, and the dull days also,
> When the soreness of lying so much in bed is over,
> When the physician, after long putting off, gives the silent
>   and terrible look for an answer,
> When the children come hurried and weeping, and the
>   brothers and sisters have been sent for,
> When medicines stand unused on the shelf, and the
>   camphor-smell has pervaded the rooms. . . .

In completing this section, the poet answers all these *whens* with the predictable, causal *then* ("Then the corpse-limbs stretch on the bed, and the living look upon them. . . . "), but this common logical pattern was by no means his favorite. Certainly Whitman, as the great American cataloger, took naturally to repetitive method of all sorts; he was crazy to get everything in, and the repeat brought unlikely things immediately together, made order, made shape, smoothed over the rough edges by the simple power of the voice repeating thus driving home widening image after image while keeping the lens tapped down and focused. It was a way, in fact, to add detail to the scene while resisting narrative sequence, resisting the forward press of *time* itself. Instead, there's that all-at-once, stopped, near eternal feel in Whitman even as we get a restless sweep, background and foreground, a complication usually supplied by *story*'s movement from one set point to another—the physician, in the passage just mentioned, then the children hurrying, the brothers and sisters coming, the medicines useless now, camphor overpowering the sick room.

The effect of these small fragments is large. Whitman's method is profoundly lyric though not particularly personal, which seems almost an oxymoron given the traditional and nearly automatic connection between the lyric impulse and the self. Of course, the sense of self, Whitman's big voice and its claims, is all over *Leaves of Grass*. The poem is famous for that. But its movement is lyric in how it affects us, the readers: we're released—not kept by the confines of *story*—allowed by the repetitions a seemingly unlimited amount of time to understand what's happening. Peter Kivy, a philosopher of music, has written how the repeats for composers and anyone who listens perform a similar "obvious and vital" function. They break up what might be a straight-out unbending temporal sequence, offering a "freedom to wander, to linger, to retrace one's steps." Or, more apt in this comparison to poetry, repeats, according to Kivy, not only enable us to "grasp" a pattern—and thus its sense—they allow us the luxury of "groping" for it, two things intertwined in any memorable aesthetic experience, the *how* and the *what*, both. Suddenly, we're inside the actual *making;* the poem or piece of music mimes that making, how the mind goes over and over things in order to order them in the first place. In Whitman's work, we see that process close up, his musing built in through the numerous ways he repeats things.

Scanning *Leaves of Grass* for one of his most common repetitive techniques is easy enough. Your peripheral vision turned low, you stare down the left margin where so often the identical declarative bits beginning each line practically explode off the page—the exuberant speaker *pleased with* women, primitive tunes, earnest words, *pleased with* the old and new. Or he's *where* the path is worn, the quail whistling, the bat flying, the cattle standing, *where* the human heart's beating, the she-whale swimming. Or there's *the law* of the past, the present, *the law* of the living, of promotion, of heroes, of drunkards. Nothing gets past this fellow or refuses him. As he likes to boast in "Song of Myself," it's

> In vain the plutonic rocks send their old heat against my
> approach,
> In vain the mastodon retreats beneath its own powder'd
> bones,
> In vain the ocean settling in hollows and the great monsters
> lying below,
> In vain the buzzard houses herself with the sky,
> In vain the snake slides through the creepers and logs,
> In vain the elk takes to the inner passes of the woods,
> In vain the razor-bill'd auk sails far north to Labrador. . . .

And so on, and on, throughout this tireless American epic. The ancestor here lies in the very oldest call-and-response rituals, the individual adding new phrases as the group answers the same way each time, creating tension through opposites: variation and theme or, closer to the bone, danger and safety. How wildly are we willing to travel in the bits that *don't* repeat before coming back to the solace of the repetition, the increasingly familiar sound? If Pound was right and all poetry, all art, is made of these two elements, the fixed and the variable, Whitman's brilliance lies in the distance he's able to wander between these two points. Here, the "in vain" is a local counter-weight against the expansive reach of image that takes us as far back in time as the mastodon, as deep in the brain as the great sea monsters that lie in wait. But it's the "in vain . . . in vain" that keeps the human pressure on—one might even say *keeps poetry on*—that intimate yet communal response that convinces and alerts us, moving us deeper into the next level of meditation and complication.

Repetition, in fact, might be too general a word and not nearly subtle enough for what happens here, since each "in vain" turns up ignited by the run of imagery before it—from rocks and mastodons through buzzards and snakes to elk and auk—images that somehow alter and enrich the seemingly identical phrase intoned as we move on. Something similar about the repeat in music, often spoken of by musicologists, Edward T. Cone among them, concerns how we hear that same melody early then late in the almost-never-strictly-followed *a-b-a* form of the sonata, which nevertheless is the starting point for so many chamber pieces and larger symphonic shapes. By the second time, in the recapitulation, it's hardly an honest-to-god repetition at all; now we're registering everything, including the "variation" that's come between these recurring themes. The context has changed, which, in fact, changes everything. So Whitman's *in vain* gets larger, more powerful as more and more things are added to the mix: the poet will—*will*—see it all.

In music, theorist Leonard Meyer makes a distinction between two kinds of repetitive method. Too many repetitions—here's where repetition makes a bad name for itself—and the mind longs for relief in variation; all those auks and mastodons and sea monsters desperately wished for now against the tedious run of *in vain, in vain*. Too few, and we're drowning in dense detail and it's way too busy. We want to be pulled back to the bottom, to some phrase that will soothe us against all this lively rattle; seen in this light, the *in vain* is solace, a home place. Either way, Gertrude Stein cut to the chase on this; I'd give her the last word any day. There's no "repetition" in genuine human expression, she wrote, only "insistence," a remark Whitman would surely have cherished, himself a poet who was nothing if not insistent, revising and republishing his *Leaves of Grass* as many times as he did. But more, invoking her old teacher from Harvard, Stein casts it all in a more elemental way. "This is what William James calls the Will to Live," she wrote. "If not," she added with high Whitmanesque drama, "nobody would live."

❧

Such urgency, that *insistence*, might color everything in poetry, this most personal of all literary forms. Kierkegaard thought it was only through repetition that we created the self at all—a major accomplishment—though certainly poetry goes further than the self, one hopes, at least to include the *other* and, in the best work, to include the world. The more I read Larry Levis's final book, *Elegy*, the more I'm struck by how powerful and complex repetition, this insistence, can be, how—William James and Gertrude Stein perhaps cheering on the thought—*life-giving* it seems even in the face of sorrow, its weave and counterweave. One feels the weight of Whitman in this posthumous collection, especially in Levis's long and intricate elegies that make up much of the book, whose inward energy, as in Whitman's work, seems about even with its outward, rhetorical force.

The opening passage of "Elegy with an Angel at Its Gate" is particularly effective in this way, the so-called "Muir in the Wilderness" section that is carefully made of just four sentences, the last threading down an astonishing forty-nine lines, the whole of it cast largely into three-line stanzas whose odd-numbered arrhythmia unsettles and pitches us forward. As with many pieces in the book, the mood is meditative unto hypnotic, faintly apocalyptic, the tiniest detail immense. The feel sometimes echoes Wallace Stevens in his last poems, which Randall Jarrell claimed were "from the other side of existence," from "someone who sees things in steady accustomedness, as we do not, and who sees their accustomedness, and them, as about to perish." These "poems," he went on, "magnanimous, compassionate, but calmly exact, grandly plain. . . ."

Repetition, the way these things go and come back, guides Levis's poem from the start. "We were the uncountable stars, at first," it begins; in fact, "we were nothing, at first," the two declarations striking a troubling balance, the heady expanse of "stars" against the leveling "nothing," then what we *never* were—"the color-blind grass . . . the pattern of the snake / fading into the pattern of the leaves." Eventually, as we move into the fourth sentence, which itself seems never to stop unfolding and turning back, things are reset and reined in by a simple phrase—"part of"—more subtle, not as predictably sequenced as Whitman's "in vain" or all his *whens whens whens* in line after line, but recurring the way a musical phrase reasserts itself just as we were dreaming off under the spell of the detail in some countermeasure. How is it that we've vanished when we were so "uncountable" at first? So runs the suggestion of a question seeded in the earlier passage that now forces an answer, made breathless by long accumulation. The poem continues in its "calmly exact" way to show how such a reversal takes place: "by becoming part / of everyone." Which is to say,

> . . . part of the horses bending
>
> Their necks to graze, part of every law,
> Part of each Apache heirloom for sale
> In a window, part of the wedding cake,
>
> Part of the smallpox epidemic, part of God,
> Part of each blind crossroad, part
> Of the ending rain turning to snow,
>
> Part of each straw in the lighted,
> Open doors of boxcars as they pass,
> Part of the wars, part of each silk piece
>
> Of lingerie, part of what can never be
> Untangled, evaluated, cross-examined. . . .

So it goes on, past lovers and the drive-in movie and the scent of linen, past the oldest trees and the "slaughterhouse with its fly-covered / Windows," all part of us now or, more humbly, we a part of them in the great vanishment. It was Frost who claimed that the overwhelming subject of poetry is always death, its shadow lurking even in the happiest of pieces. But Levis's refusal to close down this run of thought even on the most basic sentence level, forcing that cadence on and on through forty-nine lines, the dark vitality in every move to the next thing and the next thing and the next thing suggests undoubtedly the "will to live" that Stein understood even in the simplest, most awkward repetition. Yet Levis is neither simple nor awkward. How his assemblage turns both garish and vast, past irony into something more unnerving is the thing that silences.

> To be part of another, larger thing that ends
> By becoming a movie about it, the popcorn,
> The audience sitting there watching it
>
> With their mouths open, the big screen there
> In front of them, each one a part of it
> Designed to stroll languidly out
>
> Into the hot, impossible night in the city. . . .

Now the sound is the sound of conclusion, no longer the layering "part of" but the phrase wound tightly into the ongoing fleshed-out image of the movies, then out into the street, the scene transformed to *mean* in a dizzying way—"to be part of another, larger thing," he writes. Of course, we're ready for that closure as the section ends, everything slowing down and stopped by that ballast of the expanded image, hypnotized as we are unto exhaustion by the extravagance of Levis's repetitive moves.

It's deeply physical, such movement. Certainly the idea of "something larger" is expertly mimed in how this outrageous sentence plays out or, rather, plays itself out. The poem *says* and *does*,

in equal measure. So it convinces us. Which is to say, we no longer
need convincing.

~

It's something the body knows, visiting cellist Gary Hoffman is telling
us in his masterclass at Indiana University. My son and I have driven
two hours south to get here, through thunderstorms and their sudden
clearing. Now this cellist is insisting it's muscle memory, the arm
slowly absorbing the way of notes, phrases, entire movements by the
simple over and over, repeating the fingering endlessly, the intricate
bow strokes until one can play thinking no longer of the *how* and even
past the mysterious *what* to something else, wholly personal. My son
leans his head close to mine. "Correct repetition is the mother of
skill," he says, quoting a favorite piece of advice from his own cello
teacher, Eric Edberg. I think of how many times while writing a poem
I've read out loud the last line I've barely managed, or the last stanza,
again and again reading it out, hoping the repetition might lure what's
coming, hoping by the ritual to go empty and alert enough to get to
the next line, to *receive* the next line though I know that's not exactly
what these cellists mean.

On stage, Hoffman is modest and funny, somber by turns, entirely
engaging; we're totally smitten. Where did that first note come from?
he asks after a long pause, asks the young woman who has just played
for him and us Bach's prelude to the difficult and haunting Sixth Cello
Suite. She looks at him blankly. But we're blank too. I notice a few people glancing at each other. You see, it's not just you, he tells her. You're
coming into the middle of the thing. That music's been going on all
the time. You're just now hearing it, picking it up, letting it come
through you. The young woman looks puzzled. For the first time, it's
completely quiet in the room. That's spooky, my son whispers to me.

He was right. It was spooky—the dead speaking to us that way as
if nothing stops, ever. Every world continues, every voice. It's just

happenstance, or luck, that we hear it. And Hoffman went on to an array of other matters, large and small, my son writing it all down in his red notebook, but I stayed back, hopelessly mulling. Certain moments are gifts, after all, points of sudden heat for all manner of thought. Later, we might connect the dots backward and see where things began. Later, I thought about Eliot's old saw of an essay, "Tradition and the Individual Talent," though it's easy, even a mild pleasure these more populist days to look dimly upon its patrician airs and haughty notions. After all, do we really need to read every bit of Western poetry from Homer on before we've earned the right to cobble together one line of verse? Eliot's answer: well, yes. . . .

Beyond the pedantic sense of that piece—and certainly of Eliot himself—one finds some immensely useful, if eerie, things. Gary Hoffman to the young cellist that autumn day in Bloomington: Listen, it's not just you. You're coming into the middle of the thing. And Eliot? Anyone who would "be a poet past his twenty-fifth year" requires "the historical sense [which] involves a perception, not only of the pastness of the past, but its presence . . . its simultaneous existence" with our own. Repetition, then, on a massive, stranger scale beyond the repeat of line and rhythm and phrase within a single poem. One could claim that every word we ever use is a repetition, the same for any poetic shape or form, I suppose, no matter how willfully we stir it up to make it ours. Certainly a long line of love poems stands behind the one just written; all the elegies ever invented in their mix of fever and calm loom up before this one that came yesterday; whatever "emotion recollected in tranquility" we might name or long for, there were how many hundreds, thousands of poets who once worked toward similar meditative shapes and cadences? George Oppen's straightforward warning comes back: "Be careful," he wrote. "Study the words you have written for the words have a longer history than you do, and say more than you know." How many worlds are there, past and present, flooding this moment? I think there must be simpler ways to go mad.

But Eliot brings up something far more jarring and mysterious in that essay. Although obviously coming out of the early twentieth century's own culture wars, the other side headed up by his old friend Pound railing against the tedium of metronome and formula—or by Williams, insisting that poets seek a lively *spoken* cadence—Eliot's ideas, especially in what follows, strike me not so much as holding the grand old line as suggesting something truly odd, even surreal. He makes, in fact, an outrageous claim. "Our tendency," he wrote, is "to insist

> whenever we praise a poet, upon those aspects of his work in which he least resembles anyone else. . . . We dwell with satisfaction upon the poet's differences from his predecessors. . . . Whereas if we approach a poet without prejudice, we should often find that not only the best, but the most individual parts of his work may be those in which the dead poets, his ancestors, assert their immortality most vigorously.

I remember reading about Elizabeth Bishop when she was a college student first finding Gerard Manley Hopkins, her thrill over one small eccentric move of his, a personal aside, a parenthetical exclamation—"Fancy, come faster!"—right in the middle of his long, early poem "The Wreck of the Deutschland." Maybe it all depends on *which* dead poet then, *which* ancestor one chooses to repeat. At any rate, it was exactly the kind of parenthetical note to the self we recognize as Bishop's, one of the much-loved quirky trademarks of her work.

Still, the dead speaking to us seems to be something built right into the basic muscle and bone of all this, whether poets will it or not. Decisions about line breaks, for instance—half the time, one is automatically breaking the line in all the *given* ways, which is to say *on the phrase*—a communal gesture if there ever was one, the way meaning has been routinely parceled out in English, spoken or written, since the start of things. This against a more independent move to enjamb in some offbeat, deliberate way, to hold a note—so to speak—a little longer than usual for personal emphasis. That's genuine play between the dead and the living. There's surprising power, maybe even Eliot's "best" and "most individual" part of a poet's work, when one has the nerve to take up some image or idea already beat senseless into cliché or near it. I think about what Lesha Hurliman—a poet in my graduate workshop at Purdue—once did, facing down the hopelessly worn-out image of the American eagle, adding her own anguish to turn its four thousand pound drag into something freshly considered. Stopped at a traffic light, the speaker in her poem spots one in the distance "heaving its way somewhere," not at all the fierce image on county-fair t-shirts or truck-window decals. "I watched the giant struggle all the way / across my windshield," she wrote.

Repetition in any art—maybe this gets at Eliot's point about poetry—might be finally about ambition, the wish to take on certain solid and lasting things: subjects, states of mind, habits of thought that have seized human beings from the beginning. But the whole notion *is* spooky, as my son would say. I can't help it; I keep going back to that quiet hall in Bloomington, Bach's music rising out of nowhere how many centuries later, our own weird time warp, this over and over, the world repeating itself. It's an uneasy tension, past and present colliding within a personal lens. That's what silences us, that reach inward and outward, backward and forward at once, the fine, dangerous imbalance of it. And this is the risk. Wallace Stevens—who himself wasn't above taking on the great old subjects, love and death and reverie, howbeit in the most peculiar ways—wrote in a letter to a friend in 1948 that poetry was, for most people, partly a matter of "listening for echoes, because the echoes are familiar ... [wading] through it the way a boy wades through water, feeling with his toes for the bottom. The echoes," he said, "are the bottom." And the water? I imagine it deeper, barely eye-level now in the blinding afternoon, our suspension uneasy, unnerving in the darkening blue expanse of it.

THE RAGE TO REORDER

My yard is pretty small. I live on Maple Street and after that, the universe gets bigger: a medium-sized town, a medium-sized state, a country one can easily get lost in for years, oceans either way, continents, languages, and in that vast elsewhere, the moon, of course, other planets in their own thick darkness. But I watch one bird in my small backyard. Against the garage in a fit of I-don't-know-what, I once screwed in a birdshelf badly hammered together, for robins really, but English sparrows have taken it over each spring. And from the start, I noticed something curiously wrong. That sparrow, was he addled? Every April, I watch day after day as he—or she?—brings a fine litany for the nest, *stuff* in its grandest accumulation: grass, leaves, hair, sticks naturally enough, but bits of newspaper from the alley trash too, ATM receipts, tampon cardboard, carbon paper (yes, someone on my block must still use it), whatever's beak-sized, not moving, sometimes shiny; whatever, in short, can be carried in and woven, sort of woven. *Sort of*—note that last distinction.

Remember that the English sparrow is wildly misnamed, neither a sparrow nor particularly English, this most modest of finches descended from the endlessly ingenious weaver birds of Africa whose intricate nests continue to astound. A question then: why is the nest of the English sparrow—this weaver finch—such an incredible mess? Why so many trips up from the ground to add to its *messdom*? Just this: in spite of its prodigious numbers (assuring success, Darwin might claim), in spite of its English affectation and clear spunk, something's gone awry in the dimmest spiral of its genetic code. It's lost the weaver habit—what exactly to *do* with all this? But the collecting habit, the gathering part, mindlessly remains. *I need more I need more I need more.* Because? (Can a bird shrug?) And it pokes in another twig here, a candy wrapper there. Result: I look out to this huge pile-o-stuff, barely room now for the creature to squeeze in between nest and eave. Still, more bits come. *Surely this gold cellophane strip from that Marlboro pack would be a nice touch.* And somehow the nest absorbs it. It's not pretty but it will do, as coaches like to say after the badly played but winning game, squinting jubilant and worried, straight into the camera.

I don't know why this bird haunts me. There's my own bad housekeeping. Or a good house*making* as my husband fills the basement with how many cans of refried beans, diced tomatoes, a dusty force field to simplify our lives for just-in-case, for what-about-supper, a quiet reference in that gesture going back not to some Depression-era uncertainty but to our own childhood's fall-out shelter, that particularly gloomy *stay against confusion.* But I also write poems, and read far more of them than I write. And there's that thing about art, how it too is made of images, of stray bits—a wheelbarrow in the rain, a lost key or continent, a greenhouse full of roses—woven together somehow, oh pile-o-stuff, offered finally on the altar of meaning.

How does this work over a lifetime? The sparrow's outrageous need to keep doing it—to add and add, wasting little in the old intricate weaving—is perhaps a cautionary tale for poets, though William Carlos Williams's sparrow, in his poem named for the bird, is lauded for such "general truculence," its ways not even "remotely subtle," its will to survive so fierce. "The sparrow . . . / is a poetic truth / more than a natural one," Williams begins, only to end his poem with an image wafer-thin, "flattened to the pavement," this "effigy" of the bird, read as heroic as it is modest: "This was I, / a sparrow / I did my best, / farewell." Of course, the lifetime shape of such effort, this "best," involves for the poet far more than persistence, although, as is said about most things, showing up, not giving up, is half the battle.

Still, one continues to wonder darkly at the sparrow leaving behind a name and part of the globe in its evolution, not to mention the more immediate business: how it's left off forever making the useful thing also the beautiful thing. The fact is the bird's locked in what biologists call a "fixed action pattern": it *must* collect, no matter what the sketchy outcome. And something in the weaving part of that pattern, the—so to speak—make-it-art moment of it, has *unlocked*, released itself to chaos. Thus whatever the bird's vague formal intentions, there's a big comical mess under my eave. In animals, those fixed patterns are not individual but species-bound, back countless generations, whereas the human gauge for habit—if we dare make this uneasy analogy—is tiny, a single lifetime, though one could argue, I guess, a "species effect" from all those poets long under the sod or still with us, looming under certain cadences, invited there or not.

Nevertheless, here's a starting point: all makers, of nests or poems, collect and weave, collect and weave, badly or well; the two things make that third thing. Yet over time, for poets, the imagination seems a kind of Rube Goldberg machine, one's trademark style (whatever that may be) a messy assortment of semi- "fixed action patterns," though maybe an old habit unlocks because a new one—fresh imagery, a cadence, a subject—locks in, sending shock waves back through all that went before.

I'm assuming the best here, thinking in most cases poets—unlike the seemingly pathological sparrow—have more options in their transformation than just making the nest bigger, weirder, throwing off beauty and grace. It would, after all, be downright pathological itself to argue *against* development. But the *how* fascinates—the rate and degree of change over time—and beneath that, the *why* differing wildly poet to poet, Theodore Roethke's development profoundly unlike, say, Elizabeth Bishop's rethinking over so many decades. What's sure is that this quirky, sometimes painful interior negotiation comes poem by poem, year by year, guided by both will and need, those most fraternal, unidentical of brothers. Not to mention those other, more wily siblings, surprise and accident.

A more worldly factor enters here too, one that perhaps over-influences the *will* side of all this. An assumption of change from book to book seems particularly dramatic in certain generations of poets, Robert Lowell's, say, which includes Berryman and Roethke, continuing in certain later writers, James Wright, for example, or Adrienne Rich. Poets appearing more recently seem touched by this habit too, Jorie Graham, for one, whom I once heard say she waited two years, refusing to write any more of what she pointedly called "Erosion" poems, to make way for the willful departure of her third collection, *The End of Beauty;* or Louise Glück, who has written that each of her books culminates "in a conscious diagnostic act, a swearing off." For some, the press for serial dissonance takes on the wider world; Lowell's suddenly confessional *Life Studies* comes to mind, appearing midcentury at the start of a turbulent, less-than-reserved era. What might well be a gradual, natural progression has, for many, speeded up somehow, gone large-writ, in answer to a matter-of-fact assumption that this is what serious writers do: they change in a big way, or at least those who wish to be taken seriously do.

A quiet question stands at the heart of all this: Why this fierce rush to alter oneself? To what end? Is it a matter of emphatic cultural habit by now? And if change does occur, are there things that must *not* change and *what are they*? Because I fear this finally gets stranger, larger, more personal, having everything to do with who writes these poems in the first place. Story problem: if I'm given a really strong pair of binoculars and aim straight at the yard, everything distant suddenly close, specific, flooded with light—is it the same nest I see?

same yard? What about that poor sparrow, almost surreal, so much bigger, its feathers more bedraggled? And the one who watches all this? Like Alice in her Wonderland, drinking her own odd elixir, am I larger than I was, or way smaller? Exactly who is it now, looking through such a moment, fiddling awkwardly with the lens?

All this worry about individual change—maybe it's hot-wired into us, especially in America where novelty is worshipped ad nauseam, though this *given* may well be a twentieth-, now twenty-first-century peculiarity. After all, did Whitman care about development in quite this way? Beyond his initial rant against All Things British, not to mention his coming up with perhaps the most revolutionary idea in American poetry before or since, wasn't he mainly drawn until his death into meticulous revisions of his *Leaves of Grass*, to tidy and tame its radical stance? Or Dickinson. Her work seems roughly all-of-a-piece, though perhaps intensifying in the 1860s in response to the Civil War's massive toll in Amherst, a historical moment coming at the height of her powers, giving what she called her "flood subject"—death—sudden space and time.

It was Wallace Stevens who famously praised our "blessed rage for order," thereby defining poetry, if not human thought itself. But the rage to *reorder*? Or at least this current version? There are obvious targets in the twentieth century, triggers really, for this particular habit among poets. We can always blame Ezra Pound, his endlessly invoked *make it new*, which, my colleague Wendy Flory tells me, first came to us via his Canto 53, his translation of a four-character bathtub inscription made by Chinese emperor Tang the Victorious, some particularly cheerful day around 1750 B.C. or so. In any case, thanks to Pound, it's been the rallying call for almost a century. Or it was World War I, the Great War, the "war to end all wars"—hopeless misnomer—whose legend and reach still live on, everything, it is often claimed, altered after 1918, the nice dinner party shot to hell, the complete sentence ground down to fragments, our human sadness never again finite, our souls—no, there is no soul. And so we build back *up* from chaos to a formal vision that includes it, a view all local and global terrors have since buoyed up.

Certainly Pound saw a movement *from, out of, away* even before the great war, his insistence that poets favor image over abstraction (would that he had followed his own advice!), that they observe directly, refuse the redundant, that they write to the musical phrase and not the metronome: all this a leap into a riveting kind of attention. To Pound, the nineteenth century was largely a bust anyway. "A rather blurry, messy sort of period, a rather sentimentalish, mannerist sort of period. I write this with no self-righteousness, with no self-satisfaction," he wrote, up to his hips in both. But I suspect his call to arms against formulaic verse, a call the moderns—Williams, Moore, Stevens, even Eliot and Frost to some degree—took to heart, was mainly about that *first* going forward, refusing to turn back, throwing off old models. Did he really mean that one should keep changing with a similar high drama, book after book?

It may also be possible to blame Darwin for this press toward change and more change, at least Darwin of the popular view of his theory, simplified by metaphor, the "ladder" we supposedly keep rising, step by step. Which is to say that as life moves through time it becomes bigger, better, more complex: voilà! evolution! the amoeba reaching its grandest incarnation in the human being who thinks and mutters and plays baseball. No, absolutely not! Stephen Jay Gould, among others, has said. Darwin's idea of survival doesn't necessarily mean greater complication but often just a sensible adaptation to things that limit or destroy, the wise pale moth, for instance, darkening over a few generations in the gray air of the city, a clever way to camouflage. In short, we change as things around us change, an idea that explains, in part, more cultural, generational shifts such as Robert

Lowell's. More, it turns out Darwin's "progress" was not the straight-ahead rise some of us have been programmed to believe, his favorite metaphors messy as the sparrow's nest. Evolution is a "tangled bank," he wrote; it's a "branching coral" whose funny, wayward-looking appendages suggest all manner of future options.

Both ideas, adaptation and the branching coral, support a notion of Robert Frost's that keeps coming back to me: we don't *progress* at all really. It's not a matter of *better*. Instead, the overwhelming pattern of the universe is simply this: expansion and contraction. And again, this: expansion and contraction. We open and we close; we probably do it endlessly. In this way, poets accumulate image, tone, language, new ideas about structure to draw on (expand) or leave behind (con-tract) as seems useful, exciting, inevitable.

However we move (or expand, or contract), there are three more ideas to mull over as *spirit*, if not absolute law. The first, an old thought, is that genuine change is gradual. "Nature never leaps . . . no matter springs from a state of rest except through a lesser mo-tion," Gottfried Leibniz wrote around 1690. Second, there's our own version of the sparrow's "fixed action," development seen largely as a realization of potential, of becoming just more convinc-ingly whatever-we-were-from-the-start, an idea afloat in the world at least since Hegel. Finally, most useful and unnerving, a notion beloved by plant geneticists keen on something called "hybrid vigor": change occurs when elements apparently at odds, seen as opposites really, are absorbed over time. Lock that into your long-term memory (this will take several minutes, psychologists say). Contradictory elements: hold that warring thought.

∿

For now, consider this image: a row of greenhouses lit from within, off a large road or a small one. They're always at the edge of some town I'm passing en route to another town. Maybe it's fall. Maybe the radio's going in the car. These amazing angular structures float at dusk, barely pinned to the expansive field. And of course—another fixed pattern?—without thinking at all, I think of Roethke, whose family's greenhouses, locked way back in the Michigan childhood he wished decidedly to forget, touched the breakthrough poems of his second book, *The Lost Son and Other Poems*, with their singular strangeness. In turn, these images of utter stillness unlocked furious change in the lifetime of work ahead.

This is the common wisdom on Roethke that honors the absolute power of one's first *lived* imagery, that the greenhouse poems of his second book grounded him, launched him into what was genuinely his. Not that the initial book, *Open House*, published in 1941, was a failure, praised as it was by Louise Bogan for its lyricism, by Yvor Winters for its clarity and feeling, by Elizabeth Drew for its "controlled grace of movement." But the book at heart was an exercise—howbeit impressive—in the *givens*, the currency of the time: a highly conscious metaphysical feel, predictable cadence, large abstractions outweighing imagery, an overvoice-voice that knows, considers, concludes. Example—these lines that begin his poem "Silence": "There is a noise within the brow / That pulses undiminished now / in accents measured by the blood / It breaks upon my solitude."

This notion of the given currency is important; it's where everybody starts. And one does a passing job with it or not, though I suppose a few rare spirits ignore it completely. That Roethke did it well enough to earn kudos—he was someone acutely alert to matters of career—probably helped decide the future for him. But that he didn't exactly take that world by storm—according to his biographer Allan Seager, he saw the response to that first book as pretty faint praise—ensured perhaps one thing: he was forever cut loose from merely repeating himself. And as he began to work feverishly toward the greenhouse poems and the longer "Lost Son" pieces of the second book, he saw how hemmed in he had been. James Jackson, then his colleague at Bennington, has written that at this point "Ted sensed a tyranny, a drudgery, then a lethargy in the verse-forms of his own earlier practice." Add to that the excitement of finding real treasure from his past like the images from "Root Cellar" where "nothing would sleep," where

> Shoots dangled and drooped,
> Lolling obscenely from mildewed crates,
> Hung down long yellow evil necks, like tropical snakes.
> And what a congress of stinks!—
> Roots ripe as old bait,
> Pulpy stems, rank, silo-rich,
> Leaf-mold, manure, lime, piled against slippery planks.
> Nothing would give up life:
> Even the dirt kept breathing a small breath.

By this time, Roethke was deep into experiments on the line itself, which he wanted to remain "*at all moments* abloom . . . soft, fiery, and discursive all at once." Or so Jackson recalled, adding:

> His poems in their rough drafts startled me . . . by their obvious duo-structure: the legal or the logical co-existing side by side with the intuitive, the associational: the former being . . . certain abstract nouns, generalized epithets or crudely personified ideas. . . . These abstractions were at once so out-of-tune, so alien in their feel and texture . . . in the 'internal landscape' (of the poems) . . . that I can remember bursting out to him in immediate questioning or objection to their presence. To which Ted's quick reply and fairly casual defense was, "Sure, sure, but it's not going to *stay* in, for God's sake! It's just something left over from the thought stage of the piece. The thinky-thinky."

This thinky-thinky seems recycled from *Open House*, and such abstractions would return (contract, expand) in later collections, at times oppressive but in his best work pared down and cut with detailed imagery as in his poem "The Far Field" from the early 1960s, with heart-stopping mergings like this one:

> At the field's end, in the corner missed by the mower,
> Where the turf drops into a grass-hidden culvert,
> Haunt of the cat-bird, nesting place of the field mouse,
> Not too far away from the ever-changing flower-dump,
> Among tin cans, tires, rusted pipes, broken machinery—
> One learned of the eternal. . . .

Yet a far more daring move emerges in that second book's "Lost Son" poems, one related more profoundly to that "internal landscape" mentioned by Jackson. Roethke's very willful disconnect is not only from the "thinky-thinky," the controlling voice-over feel of that first book, but from his careful pattern in the greenhouse series too, those highly lyric pieces held in place by a loose cause-and-effect narrative. Certainly the "Lost Son" poems have concrete moments that echo that greenhouse imagery, drawn from riverlife, woods, weather—"I touched the ground, the ground warmed by the killdeer," the poet tells us, "The salt laughed and the stones; / The ferns had their ways. . . ." But against those solid references, Roethke often works in a lost, interior way: bizarre questions and commands, hypnotic pronouncements, dark and playful non sequiturs richly associative at best, perfectly arbitrary at worse. "What's this? A dish for fat lips?"—so begins, inscrutably, "The Shape of Fire." Or this, from the second section of "The Long Alley":

> The fiend's far away. Lord, what do you require.
> The soul resides in the horse barn.

Believe me, there's no one else, kitten-limp sister.
   Kiss the trough, swine-on-Friday,
Come to me, milk-nose. I need a loan of the quick.
   There's no joy in soft bones.

Two thoughts here. There is, I think, an expansive impulse behind any use of abstraction however badly—read *doggedly*, even *didactically*—managed, a wish simply to get bigger, to suggest larger meanings. Perhaps once this hunger is set in a poet's repertoire, as it was set by Roethke in his first book, it finds expression in other ways. (Darwin's branching coral could be the ghost pattern here.) If, for Roethke, tidy, heavy-handed lines you could practically whistle from *Open House* no longer washed, lines like "The spirit starves / when the dead have been subdued," which end his poem "Feud," the impulse to make assertions, to hear a voice emphatic and out there, nevertheless continues though in more guarded, interior ways. So we find lines like "There's no joy in soft bones" or later, still in "The Long Alley," "An eye comes out of the wave / Journey from flesh is longest." Here the *sound* of authority continues—all those good intentions of the sparrow bringing his bits to the nest—but the *sense*? Hard to say, reading line by line. Perhaps he was trusting something grander, writing Babette Deutsch in 1948, trying as modestly as he could to find reason for this thing that seemed to puzzle even him. He quoted from a recent reviewer of that second book who had applied Hopkins's idea of "illumination" to it, how such light could "withhold itself" in certain kinds of poems, hold back until "repeated readings" forced it to "explode." *There*, we might imagine him thinking, *that's what I wanted to do*.

Mention should probably be made of Roethke's many bouts with mental illness, two manic episodes and their attendant crashes before he wrote the "Lost Son" poems, and more as the years went on. His experience prompted him to read Jung, and his interest in the unconscious, in racial memory, preverbal and barely verbal states (for instance, his fascination with nursery rhymes), grew to such a point that he invited these things into poems. Personal terrors may give reason, even inevitability, to his deeply intuitive, at times bewildering moves.

For our part, we connect such statements or try to, though often it's a stretch to see this overly dream-struck, arbitrary element in Roethke as a natural move off the controlled force of *Open House*. Which, of course, is where the *will* comes in, howbeit in another guise. "Fears of the artist," a student quoted Roethke from class at the University of Washington, "once you've done a thing well, you have to do it again, but differently." If the aim is to evolve, organisms need, as the scientists tell us, to adapt, that is, to absorb "contradictory" elements like that brave moth, darkening in smog. I suspect that Roethke, in going as far as he was able to another way of working, was also honoring the famous dictum—no advance without contraries— from William Blake, a poet who meant much to him. "Plenty of times chances are taken," he wrote to Ralph Mills about the "Lost Son" pieces. "I don't say it's the only way to write, but . . . to break ground . . . (It's a civilization of objects and nutty juxtapositions)."

He kept it up; it wasn't just a momentary sideshow. He continued in this wayward, fragmented mode on and off; he wanted "tail flicks," he told Babette Deutsch, "from another world, seen out of the tail of the eye," at least through the next two books. Yet how much this willful disconnecting is finally definitive of Roethke isn't clear, unless the ease and surprise and beauty he manages between abstraction and image, between worlds in his later poetry—stunning in pieces like "The Far Field" and "Meditations of an Old Woman"—came about exactly *because* he was willing to go fast and loose and even over the top for a while. If so, when looking at the whole of his work, zeroing in on specific parts, we might do a reverse spin on his remark about the *thinky-thinky:* "It's not going to *stay* in, for God's sake!" we might hear him saying. "That's just for the fathomless who-knows-what stage of the piece that connects me to the void, the *leapy-leapy*. . . . "

∼

How much a poet needs—or is willing—to "break ground" and whether such change is genuine might be far less a matter of step-by-step decisions than we think, though boredom surely counts in the short run. It's true: we should never underestimate boredom as tool and trigger, that sick loggy feeling poets sometimes get at the sound of their own voices. (Consider Roethke once more, writing this time to Kenneth Burke, another colleague at Bennington, that he was launched into his new work because that first book seemed finally "too wary . . . dry . . . too constricted in rhythm.") What might matter more in this whole murky business of change or not-change is one's own sense of poetry, one's *ars poetica* or, as a steely-eyed, physical therapist might say, glaring down at any bad knee, one's "range of motion"—in such a moment, obviously, very bad. Roethke's *ars poetica*, his "range of motion," balanced the old, high-contrast dichotomies, the familiar back and forth of narrative/lyric, reason/intuition, abstraction/image, utter control to barely-put-a-sentence-together vulnerability. It's a thing I find myself sometimes asking poets in my classes, as a starting point: describe two opposing poles in your work, two states of mind and invention as unlike as you can imagine, two warring takes on your poems for the time you're long gone, off the planet entirely, and someone gets curious.

In some quarters, growing graceful within one's range of motion might be called "finding one's voice," a phrase that makes me as doubtful as reviewers do who insist with great energy that "Miss What's-Her-Name finally sounds like herself"—whatever that means. Gerard Manley Hopkins had a theory that points out the dangers in such thinking. Noting a recognizable voice in anyone might be a matter of figuring out that poet's "Parnassian," Hopkins's name for work made "on and from the level of a poet's mind," that is, for poems "that one could conceive oneself writing . . . if one *were* the poet," nothing truly terrible really but only deserving a second ranking. He went on, warming to the danger. "When a poet palls on us, it is because of his Parnassian. We . . . have found out his secret." It's too "characteristic" of the poet, he continued, "too so-and-so-all-overish, to be quite inspiration."

Hopkins was young, only twenty when he wrote this, years from the brilliant poems he himself would write, not even up to his own *Parnassian* yet, let alone "inspiration," the very first ranking he made for work that surprises past the "Parnassian," genius work that "sings." I suppose Hopkins's Parnassian describes the nature of one's own "given" in the end, the style, voice, manner—whatever makes up one's poetic print—worked out against the more general aesthetic of the age. And his "inspiration"? That's where poets surprise themselves and bust right through their own *givens*.

To get to such a place? Sometimes it really does surprise, and not always painlessly. Robert Lowell, years after the fact, admitted that his well-known move to a more personal subject matter and a highly vernacular phrasing in *Life Studies* had something to do with what was dizzyingly going on around him during his reading tour in California, March 1957, about a year and a half after Ginsberg first read "Howl" one night in North Beach to a wild but thoroughly reverent crowd. Lowell's visit during that electrified time, when, as he put it, even "very modest poets were waking up prophets," helped him refocus. Next to such work, Lowell remarked, "my own poems seemed like prehistoric monsters dragged down into the bog and death by their ponderous armor." Not that anyone in his right mind imagines Lowell a Beat poet. He did, after all, insist in the same breath that the "four musts" for oral performance—"humor, shock, narrative and a hypnotic voice"—weren't always a sign of "inspiration." But to widen one's range of motion? And slip out of one's Parnassian into what will become another, quite different version of it or maybe even Hopkins's honest-to-god *inspiration*? A deep, unbiased look at what seems thoroughly *other* might have this power; boom—and it's clear what one's "fixed action patterns" mean or what they, quite abruptly, no longer mean.

That a one-night stand in Ginsberg's California, even a month's worth of them, could have such force seems remarkably rare in spite of Stephen Jay Gould's lively defense of what he called *punctuated equilibrium*, an evolutionary theory in which movement toward change comes in relatively rapid fluctuations. At least concerning poetry, I suspect revelation is usually a slower creature, more in keeping with Leibniz's idea that "nature never leaps," that "no matter springs . . . except through lesser motions." Thus we're reminded of another model to treasure: change takes time, and a lot of it. One can literally *hear* this fact played out, not in poetry for a moment but in music, though it requires a look back more than a century to find it.

I'm tapping this as metaphor but the real story shines. Consider Johannes Brahms at fifty-eight—famous, praised enough, nevertheless reversing himself, rewriting, actually gutting a full third of his first piano trio, the Piano Trio op. 8, composed almost four decades earlier. It's intriguing, this capsulated version of change over time, the older Brahms's range of motion considerably expanded and contracted at once.

There were, for the record, both large and small reworkings. The smaller ones suggest certain rules writers might warm to: his dropping two lovely bits ripped off from Schubert and Beethoven (rule: don't steal); the run of semi-cheesy violin moves he banished, put in earlier for Joseph Joachim to play (rule: never write to pacify friends). As for clichés, when kept at all, he ran them through a meat grinder; in the fourth movement, for instance, his later take on a melodramatic Viennese waltz is downright demonic. As for key (key IS mood, a violinist told me recently), it took many turns, major to minor to major, though the darkening minor kept winning (rule: grief? It only gets bigger). In the end, most of the first, third, and fourth movements were rewritten though, happily, he kept the first movement's first theme, possibly the most Brahmsian of Brahms's melodies, its tone— melancholy, expansive—something carried with him from his youth in Hamburg, from the astonishing sepia beauty of that place (rule of rules: know what to keep; what continues may be more important than what changes).

A larger phantom rule underscores Brahms's revision, a new, fixed-action pattern that vastly changed his range of motion. At twenty-one, in the first version, he fell so in love with his initial theme that he repeated it, again and again through each movement, a habit that showed up in much of his early work. At fifty-eight, contrast obsessed him. Perhaps his years of orchestra work drove that, the larger canvas simply demanding that *more go on*. After all, Robert Schumann has said that his friend's best chamber works were really "veiled symphonies," which is to say, I guess, the fall of Rome *can* be etched onto a dinner plate. And here was Brahms, doing it.

This notion of contrast overwhelms not only the later version of this trio; it's largely how we see Brahms now. To quote his biographer, Hans Gal, just as ancient physics has pointed out nature's *horror vacui*, its intolerance of empty space, so Brahms eventually developed a *horror repetendi*, a dread of repetition, a principle Ezra Pound's *make it new* echoes. Which explains all the quirky sideways variation in that revised trio, explains what two musicians in my town—violinist Regan Eckstein and cellist Margo Marlatt—told me recently about playing this piece, that its "tricky tricky rhythms" sometimes mean, for the first movement especially, how "the piano is off . . . doing its spooky restless triplets" while the cello's "moving up in its gorgeous thing," and the violin, elsewhere, continues down some other complicated path. A "great, odd, three-level oblivious world," Marlatt said. Contrast enough, perhaps, for any ear.

But something larger kicks in, normal enough here to be utterly strange. It's that place, said Eckstein, where the piano suddenly "slows to nearly nothing." And for six bars, the cello and violin play alone in simple unison. "How lovely and sustained that feels," she said, "a kind of repose, after all that *stuff* going on." It's comforting somehow and rings true to me that Brahms took thirty-seven years— no rushing into anything—to know how to remake this to its wildest tangle. And then, knew exactly how to unmake it, untangle it. *Repose*, that violinist called it, taking us back to the sweet, plainest world imaginable. Of course, the larger structures in the trio do this too, Brahms's first themes, for all his digression, returning with power at the end of his movements, however darkly off balance in that trademark haunted way of his. So *resemblance*, that *come home, come home* is there. A very sane kind of beauty, however briefly, in the world.

~

Sanity. I hardly know how to think about sanity, though Brahms surely helps. I know a couple of years ago I spoke to a friend, fiction-writer Barbara Bean, over tea (or was it beer?) in her kitchen in Greencastle, Indiana, about this idea, not even an idea yet: change, the *why* of it, the *why bother*. What I really admire, she said point blank against all comers, is how certain writers mainly *stay there*. We mulled this over a while—to develop down, and deeper, an alternative *rage to reorder*, though not rage; not even, really, a reordering. By beer number two, we'd decided what is completely obvious: it was Elizabeth Bishop, our stellar example of someone who just—damn it—stayed put.

Of course, Bishop is an example of about a thousand tough, wry, heart-literate things. Though she didn't transform herself as dramatically as her friends and others in her generation—Lowell, Berryman, Roethke, though probably never Randall Jarrell had he lived—much has been said about her various changes, a whole cottage industry sprung up on the work she slowly, so carefully made. Few would argue that her progression was an opening outward and inward, and in that, a quieter version of what her peers had more wildly managed, first moving off the abstract (read: symbolic) *givens* of the time to the last books' more immediate, personal perspective, in a way also a *given* of those later decades. Still, "to slow the pacing is to expand," that violinist who played Brahms told me. Perhaps Bishop's unhurried moves through these phases—only about one hundred poems in total, cast over some forty years ("I'd have written more, I think, if I were a man," she said once to George Starbuck)—have a lot to do with what feels genuine, a fully earned sense of growth in her work, "fixed-action patterns" that remained fixed but gradually loosened, more graceful and edgy, both. Any further gathering by Bishop (à la the poor sparrow) from the world or the self was pretty much (unlike said sparrow) wisely woven in.

Bishop herself has famously *not* revealed that much about her process in these matters, though once, when she was filling in for Roethke at the University of Washington, she said she wished her students—one of whom, Wesley Wehr, recorded her remarks— would quit spending "so much time trying to 'discover' themselves," trying to "convey the truth about themselves." The truth is always revealed "despite ourselves," she went on. "It's just quite often we don't like how it turns out." Instead? "To concentrate more on the difficulties of writing good poems, all the complications of language and form." In short, looking *down*, *into*. Only then, she said, would "the truth . . . come through quite by itself."

That truth, for Bishop, took time. A favorite thing when I was a kid—the only perk in going to the dentist—were those "which one is different" pictures in old spit-mossed, dog-eared copies of *Highlights for Children* to be stared at and stared at until the weighty distinctions came clear. It's no doubt another obvious idea to put Bishop's early poem "Large Bad Picture" next to "Poem," a piece from her last book, *Geography III*, both about paintings her uncle did, though the canvases are years apart, the first managed when he was an adolescent. If one stares at these two long enough—keeping Brahms's double take on his Trio no. 8 in one's side vision—crucial things about her development come clear.

We can make short order of "Large Bad Picture," at base a description of the painting itself, a harbor—possibly the "Strait of Belle Isle" with its "receding" cliffs above the bay's "perfect waves" (a wry tip here: *perfection*, the telltale sign of all bad pictures, be they large or not). In this one, a slew of "fine black birds / hanging in *n*'s" seems exactly the way we, as children, inked them in. Certain elements of Bishop's are already set—the irony and truth of "perfect" and the arched-eyebrow, offhand notice of the ships docked there. "Apparently they have reached their destination," she tells us. Characteristic, too, is the quirky imagined sound of the *n*'s of birds, their "crying, crying," and the odder still "occasional sighing / as a large aquatic animal breathes." Strange, unseen, dreamt, this creature: so another, richer level opens, just when irony might seem to be enough.

"Poem," despite its humble title, is the far better piece, a triumph really, driven by Bishop's "fixed-action patterns" of many years—her exact observation, her trust in the image, her humor and unpretentious gravity. All live here, but even Hopkins might agree she's past such Parnassian, well into inspiration with this poem. Here, a much smaller (and finer) painting by that same uncle is observed—"About the size of an old-style dollar bill . . ." It's Nova Scotia (though there is, at first, a doubt), and Bishop draws us back to the actual-as-it-happened of the painting itself—"some tiny cows, / two brushstrokes each, but confidently cows," not to mention the wild iris, "fresh-squiggled from the tube." And birds? No longer simply the *n*'s of the earlier poem. Now one "specklike" is "flying to the left. / Or is it a flyspeck looking like a bird?" she says. It's these abrupt asides and questions and exclamations—"Heavens, I recognize the place," she says at last, "I know it!"—that loosen things further and show us her remarkable growth over so much time, her vastly more fluid movement: in, out, up, down. Here it's not only the painting; it's the poet staring down the painting that we watch. Even the flashbacks expertly take care of what might have been very dogged exposition, engaging us because we simply *overhear*. "*Would you like this?*" someone says about the painting. "*I'll probably never / have room to hang these things again.*"

Soon enough we understand that all this work is *approach*, a playful, earnest exposition. In "Large Bad Picture," Bishop's stab at deepening the level, at philosophical closure, seems forced, somewhat static, finally sort of a yawn, first just piling up adjectives—the sun in its sunset is "perpetual . . . comprehensive, consoling"—then her wondering if the ships are there for "commerce or contemplation." In "Poem," the impulse to end things in a larger sweep continues. But here the poet is *in* the poem, fully figuring things out, engaged with the place and the whole notion of art itself, the nature of the very small to the very large. "Which is which?" she asks herself and, by way of poetry's unique remote sensing device, asks us.

> Life and the memory of it cramped
> dim, on a piece of Bristol board,
> dim, but how live, how touching in detail
> —the little that we get for free,
> the little of our earthly trust. Not much.

With that glum, two-stressed "not much," Bishop inadvertently opens the gift anyway; the size of "our abidance," as she calls it, nevertheless includes riches—those cows, the iris "crisp and shivering," the "yet-to-be-dismantled elms, the geese"—a list almost unbearably delicate, exact, grief-struck. Slightly earlier in the poem Bishop, with typical modesty, turns down the high-minded word *vision* for what she sees, preferring simply to look: "'visions' is / too serious a word— our looks, two looks," she says of this lost world made by both painter and poet. It's a polite refusal hardly anyone, save Bishop herself, would believe. Maybe not even Bishop.

But the distinction is telling. At heart, this must be all anyone is after in the slow or anxious drive for what is new from book to book: a wish that one's mere looking at things—done long enough, with enough care and grace—will make way for the real vision. As for that "vision"—whatever she'd consent to call it—Bishop might have had something in mind, far closer to home than might be imagined. When interviewer Ashley Brown once asked about her friend Robert Lowell's famous transition from his early dense formal style to a personal, looser, in some sense far more flawed way with language and subject, Bishop thought for a moment. "One does miss the old trumpet blast of *Lord Weary's Castle*," she slowly admitted. "But poets have to change, and possibly the more subdued magnificence of his later tone is more humane."

Humane. I'd call that high praise.

Works Consulted

Ammons, A. R. "The Poem Is a Walk." In *Claims for Poetry*. Ed. Donald Hall. Ann Arbor: University of Michigan Press, 1982.

Andrews, Tom. *The Collected Poems of Tom Andrews*. Oberlin, Ohio: Oberlin College Press, 2002.

Aristotle. *The Basic Works of Aristotle*. Ed. Richard McKeon. New York: Random House, 1968.

Barker, Joel. *Wild Fowl Decoys*. New York: Windward Press, 1934.

Beckerman, Michael. *Dvořák and His World*. Princeton, N.J.: Princeton University Press, 1993.

Bede. *A History of the English Church and People*. Trans. Leo Sherley-Price. Revised by R. E. Latham. New York: Viking-Penguin, 1968.

Bishop, Elizabeth. *The Complete Poems, 1927–1979*. New York: Farrar, Straus & Giroux, 1983.

———. "Gerard Manley Hopkins: Notes on Timing in His Poetry." *Vassar Review* 23 (February 1934).

———. Jacket blurb for *Life Studies*, by Robert Lowell. New York: Farrar, Straus & Giroux, 1959.

———. *One Art: Letters*. Ed. Robert Giroux. New York: Farrar, Straus & Giroux, 1994.

Bly, Robert. *Selected Poems*. New York: Harper & Row, 1986.

Boland, Eavan. *In a Time of Violence*. Manchester: Carcanet, 1994.

Brahms, Johannes. *Life and Letters*. Ed. Styra Avins. Trans. Josef Eisinger and Styra Avins. New York: Oxford University Press, 1997.

Brooks, Cleanth, and Robert Penn Warren. *Understanding Poetry*. New York: Holt, Rinehart and Winston, 1950.

Brown, Ashley. "An Interview with Elizabeth Bishop." In *Elizabeth Bishop and Her Art*. Ed. Lloyd Schwartz and Sybil P. Estess. Ann Arbor: University of Michigan Press, 1983.

Coleridge, Samuel Taylor. *The Annotated Ancient Mariner*. Notes by Martin Gardner. New York: Potter, 1965.

——. *The Rime of the Ancient Mariner*. Illus. Gustave Doré. New York: Harper's, 1877.

Colles, H. C. *The Chamber Music of Brahms*. London: Oxford University Press, 1933.

Cone, Edward T. *Musical Form and Musical Performance*. New York: Norton, 1968.

Croll, M. W. "The Baroque Style in Prose." In *Studies in English Philology*. Ed. Kemp Malone and Martin B. Rund. Minneapolis: University of Minnesota Press, 1929.

Curran, Terri. "A Literary History of English" (unpublished manuscript). Providence College, Providence, R.I.

Davenport, Guy. *The Geography of the Imagination*. San Francisco: North Point, 1981.

Deleuze, Gilles, and Félix Guattari. *What Is Philosophy?* Trans. Hugh Tomlinson and Graham Burchell. New York: Columbia University Press, 1994.

Dvořák, Antonín. *Symphonies Nos. 8 and 9 in Full Score*. New York: Dover, 1984.

Edison, Thomas A. *The Diary and Sundry Observations of Thomas Alva Edison*. Ed. Dagobert D. Runes. New York: Philosophical Library, 1948.

Edson, Russell. "The Prose Poem in America." *Parnassus* 5, no. 1 (1976).

——. *The Wounded Breakfast*. Middletown, Conn.: Wesleyan University Press, 1985.

Eliot, T. S. *The Complete Poems and Prose of T. S. Eliot*. New York: Harcourt, Brace, 1952.

Euclid. *The Thirteen Books of Euclid's Elements*. Trans. Thomas L. Heath. New York: Dover, 1956.

Fischl, Viktor. *Antonín Dvořák, His Achievement*. Westport, Conn.: Greenwood, 1970.

Freud, Sigmund. *Collected Papers*. Vol. 2. Trans. Joan Riviere. London: Hogarth Press, 1949.

Frost, Robert. "' . . . getting the sound of sense': An Interview." In *Poetry and Prose*. Ed. Edward Connery Lathem and Lawrance Thompson. New York: Holt, Rinehart and Winston, 1972.

———. *The Selected Prose of Robert Frost*. Ed. Hyde Cox and Edward Connery Lathem. New York: Holt, Rinehart and Winston, 1966.

Fussell, Paul. *Poetic Meter and Poetic Form*. New York: Random House, 1979.

Gal, Hans. *Johannes Brahms, His Work and Personality*. Trans. Joseph Stein. New York: Knopf, 1963.

Ginsberg, Allen. *Collected Poems*. New York: Harper & Row, 1984.

Gioia, Dana. "Studying with Miss Bishop." *New Yorker*, Sept. 15, 1986.

Gould, Stephen Jay. *Wonderful Life*. New York: Norton, 1989.

Graham, Jorie. *The End of Beauty*. New York: Ecco, 1987.

Grimes, John. *On Surveying and Boundaries*. Indianapolis, Ind.: Bobbs-Merrill, 1922.

Gross, Harvey. *Sound and Form in Modern Poetry*. Ann Arbor: University of Michigan Press, 1968.

Hall, Donald. "Goatfoot, Milktongue, Twinbird." In *Claims for Poetry*. Ed. Donald Hall. Ann Arbor: University of Michigan Press, 1982.

———. "The Line." In *A Field Guide to Contemporary Poetry and Poetics*. Ed. Stuart Friebert and David Young. New York: Longman, 1980.

Hamilton, Ian. *Robert Lowell: A Biography*. New York: Vintage/Random House, 1983.

Hampl, Patricia. *Spillville*. Minneapolis: Milkweed, 1987.

Harrison, Hal H. *Eastern Birds' Nests*. Boston: Houghton, Mifflin, 1975.

Hopkins, Gerard Manley. *The Prose and Poems of Gerard Manley Hopkins*. New York: Penguin, 1986.

Hughes, Gervase. *Dvořák, His Life and Music*. New York: Dodd, Mead, 1967.

Hurliman, Lesha. "Sunlight and Oxygen." MFA thesis, Purdue University, 2002.

Jarrell, Randall. *The Complete Poems*. New York: Farrar, Straus & Giroux, 1969.

———. *Poetry and the Age*. New York: Farrar, Straus & Giroux, 1953.

———. *Randall Jarrell's Letters*. Ed. Mary Jarrell. New York: Houghton, Mifflin, 1985.

———. *The Third Book of Criticism*. New York: Farrar, Straus & Giroux, 1965.

Junck, Robert. *Brighter Than a Thousand Suns: A Personal History of the Atomic Scientists*. Trans. James Cleugh. New York: Harcourt, Brace, 1958

Kees, Weldon. *The Collected Poems*. Lincoln: University of Nebraska Press, 1975.

Kenyon, Jane. *New and Selected Poems*. St. Paul: Graywolf, 1997.

Kierkegaard, Søren. *Repetition: An Essay in Experimental Psychology*. Trans. Walter Lowrie. New York: Harper & Row, 1964.

Kivy, Peter. *The Fine Art of Repetition*. New York: Cambridge University Press, 1993.

Klee, Paul. *Paul Klee: The Thinking Eye*. London: Lund Humphries, 1961.

Kohut, Heinz, and Siegmund Levarie. "On the Enjoyment of Listening to Music." In *Psychoanalytic Explorations in Music*. Ed. Stuart Feder et al. Madison, Wisc.: International Universities Press, 1990.

Lamb, Charles. *The Letters of Charles Lamb*. London: J. M. Dent, 1945.

Larkin, Philip. *Collected Poems*. London: Noonday, 1989.

Leibniz, Gottfried. *New Essays on Human Understanding*. Trans. Peter Remnant and Jonathan Bennett. New York: Cambridge University Press, 1981.

Levertov, Denise. *Relearning the Alphabet*. New York: New Directions, 1970.

Levis, Larry. *Elegy*. Pittsburgh, Pa.: University of Pittsburgh Press, 1997.

Lewis, G. Malcolm. "The Origins of Cartography." In *The History of Cartography*. Ed. J. B. Harley and David Woodward. Chicago: University of Chicago Press, 1987.

Lowell, Robert. "On Robert Lowell's 'Skunk Hour.'" In *The Contemporary Poet as Artist and Critic*. Ed. Anthony Ostroff. Boston: Little, Brown, 1964.

———. *Selected Poems*. New York: Farrar, Straus & Giroux, 1988.

Mariani, Paul. "The Satyr's Defense: Williams' 'Asphodel.'" *Contemporary Literature* 14 (1973).

McGrath, Campbell. *American Noise*. New York: Ecco, 1993.

Meyer, Leonard B. *Emotion and Meaning in Music*. Chicago: University of Chicago Press, 1957.

Mitchell, Roger. "Some Thoughts on the Line." *Ohio Review* 38 (1987).

Moore, Marianne. *The Complete Poems*. New York: Macmillan/Viking, 1981.

Neruda, Pablo, and César Vallejo. *Selected Poems*. Ed. Robert Bly. Trans. Robert Bly, John Knoepfle, and James Wright. Boston: Beacon, 1971.

Nicolaïdes, Kimon. *The Natural Way to Draw: A Working Plan for Art Study*. Boston: Houghton Mifflin, 1941.

Niemann, Walter. *Brahms*. New York: Tutor, 1937.

Olson, Charles. "Projective Verse." In *Human Universe*. Ed. Donald Allen. New York: Grove, 1967.

Oppen, George. "Selections from George Oppen's Daybook." *Iowa Review* 18, no. 3 (1988).

Oppenheimer, Paul. *The Birth of the Modern Mind: Self, Consciousness, and the Invention of the Sonnet*. New York: Oxford University Press, 1989.

Perillo, Lucia. *The Oldest Map with the Name America: New and Selected Poems*. New York: Random House, 1999.

Peterson, Roger Tory. *A Field Guide to the Birds*. Boston: Houghton Mifflin, 1939.

Plath, Sylvia. *The Collected Poems*. New York: Harper, 1981.

Pound, Ezra. *Literary Essays*. New York: New Directions, 1935.

———. *Selected Poems*. New York: New Directions, 1957.

Ricks, Christopher. *Tennyson*. New York: Macmillan, 1972.

Ridley, Mark, ed. *Evolution*. New York: Oxford University Press, 1997.

Roethke, Theodore. *The Collected Poems*. New York: Doubleday, 1975.

———. *Selected Letters of Theodore Roethke*. Ed. Ralph Mills Jr. Seattle: University of Washington Press, 1968.

———. "Some Remarks on Rhythm." In *On the Poet and His Craft: Selected*

Prose of Theodore Roethke. Seattle: University of Washington Press, 1963.

Seager, Allan. *The Glass House: The Life of Theodore Roethke*. New York: McGraw-Hill, 1968.

Simic, Charles. "Some Thoughts about the Line." In *A Field Guide to Contemporary Poetry and Poetics*. Ed. Stuart Friebert and David Young. New York: Longman, 1980.

Simmel, Georg, et al. *Essays on Sociology, Philosophy and Aesthetics*. Ed. Kurt H. Wolff. New York: Harper, 1965.

Šourek, Otakar. *The Orchestral Works of Antonín Dvořák*. Prague: Artia, 1957.

Stafford, William. *New and Selected Poems*. St. Paul: Graywolf, 1998.

Starbuck, George. "'The Work!': A Conversation with Elizabeth Bishop." In *Elizabeth Bishop and Her Art*. Ed. Lloyd Schwartz and Sybil P. Estess. Ann Arbor: University of Michigan Press, 1983.

Stein, Gertrude. *Lectures in America*. New York: Vintage, 1975.

Stevens, Wallace. *The Letters of Wallace Stevens*. Ed. Holly Stevens. New York: Knopf, 1966.

Stevenson, Anne. *Elizabeth Bishop*. New York: Twayne, 1966.

Stresemann, Erwin. *Ornithology from Aristotle to the Present*. Cambridge, Mass.: Harvard University Press, 1975.

Summers-Smith, J. Denis. *The Sparrows*. Staffordshire, England: T. & A. D. Poyser, 1988.

Sze, Mai-Mai. "Mustard Seed Garden Manual of Painting." In *The Tao of Painting*. Vol. 2. New York: Pantheon, 1956.

Tibbetts, John C. *Dvořák in America, 1892–1895*. Portland, Ore.: Amadeus Press, 1993.

Tranströmer, Tomas. *Selected Poems, 1954–1986*. New York: Ecco, 1987.

Weaver, Mike. *William Carlos Williams: The American Background*. New York: Cambridge University Press, 1971.

Wehr, Wesley. "Elizabeth Bishop: Conversations and Class Notes." *Antioch Review* 39, no. 3 (Summer 1981).

Werner, Marta L. *Emily Dickinson's Open Folios: Scenes of Reading,*

Surfaces of Writing. Ann Arbor: University of Michigan Press, 1996. Plate A743.

Whitehead, Alfred North. *Science and the Modern World*. New York: New American Library, 1925.

Whitman, Walt. *Leaves of Grass*. New York: Dutton, 1971.

——. *Specimen Days*. New York: Signet, 1961.

Williams, William Carlos. *Autobiography*. New York: Random House, 1951.

——. *The Embodiment of Knowledge*. New York: New Directions, 1974.

——. *Paterson*. New York: New Directions, 1963.

——. *Pictures from Breughel and Other Poems*. New York: New Directions, 1962.

——. *Selected Essays*. New York: Random House, 1954.

——. *Selected Letters*. New York: McDowell, Obolensky, 1957.

——. *Selected Poems*. New York: New Directions, 1969.

Wordsworth, William. *Selected Poems and Prefaces*. Boston: Houghton Mifflin, 1965.

Zweig, Paul. *Walt Whitman: The Making of a Poet*. New York: Basic, 1984.

Index

Ammons, A. A.: "The Poem Is a Walk,"
    56, 60
Andrews, Tom: "In the Twentieth
    Century," 123–128
Aristotle, 27

Bachelard, Gaston: *The Poetics of Space,*
    120
Bean, Barbara, 199
Bede, 31–32
Beethoven, Ludwig van, 150, 169, 197
Berryman, John, 13, 186, 199
Bishop, Elizabeth, 151–163, 186, 199–
    203; "Arrival at Santos," 71, 153–155;
    "Crusoe in England," 161; "The End
    of March," 115–121; and Hopkins, 59,
    181; "In the Waiting Room," 162–163;
    "Large Bad Picture," 200–202; and
    Robert Lowell, 153, 203; and Marianne
    Moore, 158, 160–161; "The Moose,"
    58–61, 63, 155–157; "One Art," 157,
    170; "Over 2,000 Illustrations and a
    Complete Concordance," 159–160;
    "Poem," 200–203; on poetic process,
    59, 158–159, 163, 200; "Santarém,"
    151; "The Shampoo," 157
Blake, William, 194
Bly, Robert, 83; "Driving Toward the Lac
    Qui Parle River," 55
Bogan, Louise, 190
Boland, Eavan: "Anna Liffey," 33–34

Brahms, Johannes: "Piano Trio, op. 8,"
    197–199, 201
Brooks, Cleanth, 5, 14
Brown, Ashley, 203
Buffon, George-Louis, 30

Caedmon, 31–32, 34
Coleridge, Samuel Taylor: *The Rime
    of the Ancient Mariner,* 34–36
Cone, Edward T., 175
Croll, M.W., 158
Curie, Marie, 42–43, 45

Darwin, Charles, 183, 188–189, 193
Davenport, Guy, 58
Deering, Dorothy, 3
Deflaun, Pat, 165
Deleuze, Gilles, 5
Deutsch, Babette, 193, 194
Dickens, Charles, 146
Dickinson, Emily, 1, 15, 187
Doré, Gustave, 34–35
Drew, Elizabeth, 190
Dvořák, Anton: *Carnival,* 135; compari-
    son with Whitman, 137–138, 140–141,
    144, 145–146, 148–149; life in America,
    132–133, 142–143; *Symphony #9,* 131–
    137, 139–140, 144, 147–149

Eckstein, Regan, 198–199, 200
Edberg, Eric, 179

Edison, Thomas, 1–5

Edson, Russell: "My Head," 75–80; "The Prose Poem in America," 78

Eliot, T.S., 47, 182, 188; "Tradition and the Individual Talent," 180–181

Emerson, Ralph Waldo, 22, 138

Euclid, "Elements," 7

Fisher, Williams Arms: "Goin' Home," 147–148

Flory, Wendy, 187

Frost, Robert, 7, 10, 178, 188, 189

Fussell, Paul, 170–171

Gal, Hans, 198

Getty, Margaret: *Parables from Nature,* 110

Ginsberg, Allen, 69, 70, 196–197; "The Green Automobile," 64

Glück, Louise, 186

Gould, Stephen Jay, 188, 197

Gross, Harvey, 166

Guattari, Felix, 5

Hall, Donald, 7, 70, 80

Herbert, George: influence of, on Elizabeth Bishop, 59, 158

Hoffman, Gary, 179–180

Hopkins, Gerard Manley, 9, 56, 59–60, 193, 195–196, 201; and Robert Bridges, 95; "Epithalamion," 93–99; influence of, on Elizabeth Bishop, 59, 158, 181; "The Wreck of the Deutschland," 181

Hurliman, Lesha: "I Was Stopped at a Traffic Light," 182

Jackson, James, 191–192

James, William, 175, 176

Jarrell, Randall, 27, 160, 199; "Field and Forest," 101–106; "The Lost Children," 27–29; "Next Day," 29–30; on Wallace Stevens, 176; on Walt Whitman, 57, 61, 68

Jung, Karl, 193

Justice, Donald: on Weldon Kees, 67

Kees, Weldon: "Travels in North America," 67–69

Kenyon, Jane: "The Sick Wife," 61, 62–63, 66

Kierkegaard, Sören, 176

Kitterman, Susan, 131, 134, 139, 141, 149

Kivy, Peter, 173

Klee, Paul, 1, 9, 14

Kohut, Heinz, 166

Lamb, Charles, 35

Larkin, Philip: "Toads Revisited," 167–170, 171

Leibniz, Gottfried, 189

Levarie, Siegmund, 166

Levertov, Denise, 16; "An Embroidery (IV) Swiss Cheese," 107–114; *Relearning the Alphabet,* 114; *Tesserae,* 114

Levis, Larry: *Elegy,* 176; "Elegy with an Angel at Its Gate," 176–179

Lewis, G. Malcolm, 8

Lowell, Robert, 153, 188–189, 199; on John Berryman, 13; and Elizabeth Bishop, 153, 203; *Life Studies,* 13, 186, 196; *Lord Weary's Castle,* 203; "The Quaker Graveyard in Nantucket," 13; and Theodore Roethke, 89; "Skunk Hour," 13–14, 15; and William Carlos Williams, 13

Mariani, Paul, 50

Marlatt, Margo, 198–199

McGrath, Campbell: "Almond Blossoms, Rock and Roll, the Past Seen as Burning Fields," 65–66, 68

Meyer, Leonard, 175

Mills, Ralph, 194

Mitchell, Roger, 11

Moore, Marianne, 158, 160–161, 188
Mustard Seed Garden Manual of Painting, The, 15

Neruda, Pablo: "Melancholy Inside Families," 81–86
Nicolaides, Kimon: *The Natural Way to Draw: a Working Plan for Art Study*, 17
Niepokuj, Mary, 167

Olson, Charles: "Projective Verse," 16–17
Oppen, George, 180
Oppenheimer, J. Robert, 38, 46
Oppenheimer, Paul, 4

Perillo, Lucia: "The Northside at Seven," 64–65
Peterson, Roger Tory: *A Field Guide to the Birds*, 21, 23, 32
Plath, Sylvia, 26; "Cut," 5; "Elm," 5–7
Plato, 7, 36, 38
Porter, Cole: "Night and Day," 171
Pound, Ezra, 14, 48, 166, 174, 181, 187–188, 198

Rexroth, Kenneth: on Weldon Kees, 67
Rich, Adrienne, 13, 186
Roethke, Theodore, 9–11, 17, 186, 199; "The Far Field," 63–64, 192, 194; "Feud," 193; "Frau Bauman, Frau Schmidt, and Frau Schwartze," 87–92; "The Long Alley," 192–193; "Long Live the Weeds," 9; "The Lost Son," 10–11; *The Lost Son and Other Poems*, 10, 90–91, 190–194; and Robert Lowell, 89; "Meditations of an Old Woman," 194; *Open House,* 9, 90, 190,192, 193, 194; "Root Cellar," 191; "The Shape of Fire," 192; "Silence," 190

Schumann, Robert: on Brahms, 198
Seager, Allan, 190

Simic, Charles, 7, 17
Simmel, Georg, 70
Stafford, William, 66; "Traveling through the Dark," 61–62, 63
Starbuck, George, 200
Stein, Gertrude, 175, 176, 178
Stevens, Wallace, 165, 176, 182, 187, 188
Stevenson, Anne, 163
Swinburne, Algernon Charles, 171

Tennyson, Alfred Lord: "The Passing of Arthur," 3
Thoreau, Henry David, 22
Tranströmer, Tomas: "Further In," 55

Virgil, 70

Warren, Robert Penn, 5, 14
Weaver, Mike, 40
Wehr, Wesley, 200
Whitehead, Alfred North: *Science and the Modern World*, 39–40
Whitman, Walt, 56–58, 64, 69, 83, 126, 132, 174–175, 177, 187; comparison with Dvořák, 137–138, 140–141, 144, 145–146, 148–149; *Leaves of Grass*, 57–58, 68, 172–174, 187; *Memoranda*, 26; musical influences, 138–139; "Song of Myself," 22–24, 57, 138–139, 140–141, 174; "Song of Occupations," 139; "Song of the Open Road," 67; "To a Locomotive in Winter," 59, 133
Williams, William Carlos, 13, 14, 37–52, 181, 188; "Asphodel, that Greeny Flower," 41, 43–51; "The Drunk and the Sailor," 47; *The Embodiment of Knowledge,* 39–40; and Lowell, 13; *Paterson*, 41–45, 51; "Poetry as a Field of Action," 37–38, 47, 51; "The

Williams, William Carlos *(continued)*
  "The Sparrow," 184–185, "To Elsie," 68
Winters, Yvor, 10, 190
Wordsworth, William, 34–35, *Lyrical
  Ballads*, 35; ". . .Tintern Abbey," 56

Wright, James, 13, 83, 186

Yeats, William Butler, 4, 91, 126

Zweig, Paul, 58, 146

MARIANNE BORUCH is the author of five poetry collections, including *Poems New and Selected,* published by Oberlin College Press in 2004. A previous essay collection, *Poetry's Old Air,* appeared in 1995 in the "Poets on Poetry" series, University of Michigan Press. Her essays and poems have appeared in *The New Yorker, The Nation,* the *Iowa Review, American Poetry Review,* the *Massachusetts Review, Best American Poetry,* and elsewhere. Her awards include fellowships from the National Endowment for the Arts and Pushcart Prizes. Since 1987, she has taught in the graduate and undergraduate creative writing program at Purdue University, and often at the MFA Program for Writers at Warren Wilson College. She lives with her husband in West Lafayette, Indiana.